Esther Herr and Marion Nickig

Garden
Flowers from A to Z

➤ The most beautiful plants for lush,
   beautiful blooms
➤ Attractive combinations for every location

BARRON'S

Contents

Selecting Plants

Plant Portraits

Plant Arrangements

Appendix

Selecting Plants

For lush flowerbeds and borders
you need one thing above all
else: plants! The right ones for
your garden can be found in
an ever-increasing variety
of flowering beauties.

Plenty to Choose From

A garden lives principally through blooming plants. A huge selection of plants are available covering every taste, location, and requirement for care. And every year a new assortment of varieties is added to the old, familiar ones. There are essentially three plant groups to choose from, and we will introduce you to them in detail through more than 200 portraits.

Perennials

Winter-hardy perennials are among the best loved garden plants, for they reliably bloom anew every year—and usually without any great care, as long as they are in the right location (→ Extra Tip). The time for blooming varies widely and can extend through practically the whole year.

Most varieties retire to the soil in the winter; that is, their stalks and leaves turn yellow and brown. They don't grow again until spring. There are also evergreen and wintergreen varieties, plus others that draw back early in the year and leave empty spaces.

You should observe this rhythm of life as you plan your flowerbed. You should also remember that depending on the variety, perennials may take a few years to reach their full glory.

Annuals and Biennials

These short-lived garden flowers are different from perennials in that they must be seeded or planted anew every year. Annuals, in contrast to perennials, take only a few weeks to develop from

Foxglove varieties (in this case *Digitalis purpurea*) usually are short-lived.

EXTRA TIP

Living Areas
In the wild, perennials slip into the most unusual places.
The closer the location of the garden approximates this natural living area, the longer the plants will live and thrive.
Many nurseries therefore specify in their catalogs the most
promising locations—in the moist edge around water or in
the cool shade of wooded areas—for all the varieties they
sell (→ Addresses, p. 255).

a seed to a fully grown, blooming plant. Biennials need a little longer. In the year in which they are planted, they form only a rosette of leaves and don't bloom until the following year.

The blooming season of annuals and biennials generally stretches over the entire summer, so they are also referred to as summer bloomers (exceptions: spring bloomers such as Oxeye Daisy and Forget-Me-Not).

Many plants in this group last for several years in their warmer indigenous areas. In some climates, though, it is often too demanding to keep them frost-free during the winter.

Bulb and Tuber Plants

At first glance, the plants in this group don't seem to have anything in common. A springtime crocus and a dahlia, for example, could hardly be more different: the one is winter hardy, grows to a size of only a few centimeters, blooms briefly between snow and ice, and fades for the rest of the year. The other ventures forth only after mid-May and grows to over three feet.

It displays its conspicuous, colorful, and shapely blooms for several weeks before it needs to spend the winter in a frost-free cellar. The thing that unites all these flowers is buried underground: the bulbs, tubers, or rhizomes.

A springtime garden without bulb flowers is unthinkable.

Hosta likes to be in the shade—as does spurge.

The Right Choice

Every gardener has a different idea of how to arrange the garden, which plants and materials, and which colors and shapes to incorporate. But before you get too creative (→ Chapter 3), you should carefully consider your garden and yourself.

Light and Shade

Whether a plant, as presented in a catalog, grows to a height of three feet or remains uncharacteristically small; whether it is hardy and long-lived or continually sickly; whether it continually develops, stagnates, or even shrinks—all this depends primarily on the location.

The light conditions are a decisive factor: a variety that likes the shade will not give you any joy if it's placed in the sun, and the converse is also true. Whether shade, partial shade, or sun, the amount of light a plant needs is specified in the individual profiles under the key word *Location* (→ Explanations of Symbols Used on p. 25). Now you merely need to closely observe the location where you want to put your flowerbed. Determine when and how long it is in the sun in the course of a day and a year. A partially shady location should also get some strong sun—just not in the heat of midday.

In addition, note the elements that might influence the natural light and warmth conditions. For example, on sunny days is it much warmer in front of a massive wall than in front of a hedge?

The Soil

The composition of the soil is just as important as the light conditions. Most plants prefer fine, crumbly, loose, porous soil that doesn't dry out too quickly or tend to accumulate standing water. In addition to these "normal" soils, some varieties want to be in a dry location, and others need a continually moist substrate for optimal development.

Within certain bounds—as long as it's not too costly—it is possible to improve "poor" soils considerably. You can drain very damp soils (→ Technical Terms) to remove water from them. The water

> The right soil is just one criterion for good growth.

EXTRA TIP

The Crumble Test
Take a handful of your garden soil from several places about 8 inches (20 cm) deep. First roll the dirt up into a ball, and then into increasingly thin sausages; the quicker it comes apart and resists rolling, the higher the sand content. If the clumps don't disintegrate when they are rolled, they contain a lot of clay.

retention ability of excessively light, sandy soils can be improved with compost. It's easy to determine if the soil in your garden is especially permeable (sandy soil) or compressed (clay soil), rocky, or high in humus. First conduct a crumble test (→ Extra Tip) to determine what type of soil you have. You can get test strips in specialty shops to determine the pH (→ Technical Terms) or the approximate nutritional content of the soil. If you want to know precisely, have a soil sample analyzed in a laboratory.

Additional Selection Criteria

The choice of plants for a garden also depends on the size of the plot. The larger the plot is, the greater the chance of satisfying all requirements becomes. But it frequently happens that there is little room for a flowerbed. This also has an effect on the choice of plants.

Not only are large, lush perennials in small beds or gardens overwhelming, but many varieties simply have no place in a bed that's not of a certain minimum size. With mixed borders (→ Technical Terms) and perennial borders, it is especially important to plant several varieties behind one another. That's the only way to keep your bed in continual bloom, when individual plants take a break. To accomplish this, you should have a minimum width of 5 feet (1.5 m).

One further selection criterion is the toxicity of certain plants. Families with small children especially will want to avoid poisonous plants in the garden.

In choosing plants, you should also keep in mind how much time you are willing or able to invest in caring for the garden.

The size when full-grown plays a role in selecting plants.

A lush English perennial border, for example, looks very impressive and beautiful, but it involves a lot of work. Even gardens with exotic plants require much more effort than beds with plants that feel at home without much bother in a moderate climate.

The various plant groups entail the following tasks:

➤ **Annuals** have to be planted and cleaned up every year. They need regular watering and fertilizing throughout the summer.

> **Established perennials need some further watering and weeding.**

Varieties that have trouble standing on their own need to be staked.

➤ With **perennials** there is one major pruning per year, preferably in the spring. Some types need to be cut earlier (Advice in the Plant Portraits), for then they form more tubers for surviving the winter. A few varieties need winter protection in the form of brush or

Dahlias are sensitive to frost, and the tubers have to be removed from the soil in the fall.

leaves, and tall plants that are subject to falling over need support.

One application of fertilizer per year generally suffices, preferably at the time of sprouting or shortly before blooming. With most plants, watering is appropriate only during fairly long, dry periods.

➤ **Winter-hardy bulb and tuber plants** require very little care; you need to intervene only when types that are prone to running wild become too spread out.

Trim fading leaves when they turn brown and the nutrients have migrated from the leaves to the bulbs.

➤ **Bulb and tuber plants that are sensitive to frost** must be removed from the ground in the fall. In most cases, they must be dried and stored for the winter in a cool but frost-free location.

EXTRA TIP

Proper Cutting Yields More Blooms
Proper cutting can cause some perennials to bloom for a second time (e.g., sage and delphinium). The young shoots are shortened to about the width of a hand when they start to fade. A couple of weeks later they form new buds and bloom again. With varieties that flower in the fall, you can delay the blooming by cutting back the stalks by about a third at the end of June. The positive side effect is that they develop more offshoots, and consequently more blooms.

Where to Shop for Plants

Purchasing plants at the right place and the right time is a good start for a flower garden.

If you already have specific desires and ideas, the best course is to buy the plants from a nursery. You can find summer flowers and perennials at any business that sells ornamental plants. There are also special perennial nurseries that offer very large selections.

The quality in a gardening center is comparable to a nursery, but the selection of plants is limited and very seasonally oriented. Also, the varieties are not always clearly indicated. For example, sometimes you will find only a blue sage and won't know about the dark blue, spreading May Night variety or the lighter, erect Meadow Sage. On the other hand, in a perennial nursery the individual varieties are clearly identified. In addition, you can get most varieties outside the peak season.

If you are looking for a specific plant, or special seeds, and there is no source nearby, you may also take advantage of the Internet. In addition to their catalog, may nurseries offer an online shop and shipping all over the country. In addition, there have been established plant and seed dealers on the Internet for many years.

Even ordering seeds and plants from overseas is no longer a problem nowadays. However, you should not underestimate the shipping charges, which sometimes are high. In addition, in contrast to buying your plants in person at a nursery

When you buy your plants, you should inspect them carefully.

or a gardening center, you can't ask questions.

Especially at blooming time, garden flowers are offered in great variety.

When to Buy

Perennials are available practically year-round. They are sold in pots and have a compact root ball, which facilitates, in theory anyway, planting them in the flowerbed—at least as long as the ground is not frozen. The assortment available in nurseries is the greatest in the spring (April through June) and in the fall (September/October). These months are neither too cold nor too hot and generally are best suited to new plantings. Still, some plants have individual preferences, which are mentioned in the plant portraits.

In theory, perennial seeds are offered for sale all year long; however, the peak season is in the months of December through March.

Annual summer flowers can be purchased as young

plants or grown from seed. Seeds are planted right in the flowerbed, but only after thc thrcat of hard frost has passed. If you want the flowers to appear in May, you can start the plants in bowls and pots indoors as early as February or March. The seeds are bought when they are needed for starting the plants, that is, in February and March—or in the early spring, if you want to sow them in the flowerbed.

It's not worth starting some varieties yourself because the plants have very specific requirements, or because it takes them too long to grow into blooming plants. It's better to buy them as young plants in April or May. Bulbs and tubers generally are purchased dried: the spring flowering plants in the fall, when they need to be planted, and the fall flowering plants in the summer. Some varieties are marketed in pots at blooming time. They can be transplanted right away.

Recognizing Quality

When you buy plants, make sure that they are healthy, branched, and growing. Avoid buying plants
➤ with soft, excessively long, contorted shoots;
➤ with parasitic infestation or peculiar spots;
➤ with weak or decaying roots.

In addition, you should buy no perennials that have been forced to bloom quickly. They are suited only for presentation on the sales counter; they are very sensitive and short-lived.

Perennials that are raised properly will also be hardy in your garden. They may not look as fresh, green, and spic and span as the short-cultured ones, but they will flourish. In addition, they bloom later, and their pots will be filled with roots.

Annuals and biennials are easy to grow from seed.

The Convenience of Growing Your Own Summer Flowers from Seed

It's worthwhile to grow summer flowers from seed. It's easiest when you can sow the seeds right into the flowerbed without having to start them indoors. The advantage: seeds are significantly cheaper, and you get many more plants from them. After blooming, you can also harvest your own seeds for the following season. However, they may not be true to kind (see Technical Terms).

With bulbs and tubers, you should always select the largest plants. A large bulb indicates a well-stocked storehouse of nutrition from which the plant will draw its strength for growth. That means that the plants are more vital and that the flowers will be larger. Naturally, bulbs and tubers also need to be undamaged, dry, and firm.

Technical Terms from A to Z

➤ Clay soil

A very heavy, cold soil that compacts quickly with lots of moisture and "cracks" in dry conditions. It is very difficult to work. Clay soil can be shaped into soft clumps in the hand. Loosen up this soil with regular additions of sand and compost. In serious cases, it must be →drained.

➤ Cuttings

One form of vegetative propagation. Cut growth tips or stalks that are neither excessively young (very soft) or old (woody) and place them in potting soil. They will root with the aid of consistent warmth and elevated humidity.

➤ Direct seeding

Planting the seeds right in the appropriate location without first starting them in boxes, flats, or pots.

➤ Dividing

Reproducing perennials can be reproduced →vegetatively through dividing. This simultaneously rejuvenates them and stimulates them to produce more flowers. The cluster is removed from the ground, and divided with shears or a knife into fist-sized parts, which are then replanted.

➤ English country garden

Garden distinguished by a formal ground plan (i.e., by straight pathways and geometric flowerbeds that are filled with lots of plants, especially perennials). These borders generally tend to be carefully clipped hedges and are laid out in specific colors and shapes. In addition, the garden is divided into several "rooms."

➤ Family

A group of plant species with similar characteristics.

➤ Formal garden style

Garden that typically features straight lines and geometrical shapes. Planting is reserved; leafy plants frequently set the tone. At conspicuous locations and intersections of paths there are striking figures or classical decorative objects. Trimmed hedges, lawns, and gravel surfaces complete the peaceful setting.

➤ Generative propagation

Reproduction of plants sexually through seeds. This produces young plants with varying characteristics of both parent plants. In propagating plants, this circumstance is put to use to develop new varieties. In the garden, there is a danger that various varieties will cross and seed themselves, so that the originally pure plant disappears.

➤ **Genus**
The first part of a botanical name is the genus. It distinguishes various plant types that are grouped together into a genus on the basis of common characteristics. The genus name is always written with a capital letter and in italics.

➤ **Group**
Plants that resulted from the same cross and correspond to one or more breeding goals (e.g., leaf or flower shape).

➤ **Hybrid**
A genus, species, or variety that resulted from the cross between two different plants; in the botanical name it is often designated with an ×. *Salvia × sylvestris*, for example, is a species that resulted from a cross between *S. nemorosa* and *S. pratensis*. Hybrids can usually reproduce only → vegetatively, for otherwise they lose their uniformity.

➤ **Light germinators**
Plants whose seeds germinate better, or exclusively, in the light. Their seeds must not

be covered with dirt after sowing, in contrast to most other plants, which are dark germinators.

➤ **Loamy soil**
Loamy soil consists of sand, humus, and clay in specific proportions. This fertile type of soil is good for storing water and nutrients. Ventilation is generally good, especially in loamy soils with a high sand content. You can recognize this type of soil by squeezing a sample your hands: it crumbles rather than sticks together.

➤ **Mixed borders**
In contrast to a pure perennial border, several plant groups that are combined with one another—perennials, summer flowers, bulb- and tuber plants, and even shrubs.

➤ **Offshoots**
Side sprouts that grow above or below ground and that may grow out from the base of the stem, the leaf cluster, or the root ball. They may form their own roots, but they generally remain connected to the original plant. Many perennials spread through such runners. You can divide rooted plants from the base and

thus reproduce the plants →vegetatively, preferably during peak summer. Plants that send out too many offshoots can be held in check only by digging them up or by means of a root barrier.

➤ **pH**
A designation of soil acidity. Use a dipstick (e.g., from a drugstore) that changes color to measure the acidity. You can check the pH on a scale: between 0 and 7 the ground is acidic; around 7 it is neutral; and between 7 and 14 the soil is basic or alkaline. This is usually synonymous with a high lime content, which many plants don't like.

➤ **Sandy soil**
Soil distinguished by its permeability to air and water. As a result, its nutrient content is also low. Sandy soils are recognizable because they crumble in your hand. Compost can be added to increase the humus content.

➤ **Second bloom**
This occurs when a perennial that has been completely deadheaded after the first blooming grows back and develops a second, usually less robust bloom.

➤ **Self-seeding**
Many perennials, summer flowers, and bulb- and tuber plants spread their own seeds—if they are allowed to mature, without cutting off blooms—and thus develop new plants. These often are short-lived varieties, and this is the only way to keep them present in the garden. Some varieties keep spreading in this way.

➤ **Series**
A group of varieties with common characteristics that are distinguished from one another only by the color of the flowers. It is most commonly encountered in plants for balconies and flowerbeds.

➤ **Staking**
Providing support for tall plants that tend to fall over. Stores offer flexible plastic, wood, or galvanized steel supports. You can also simply put gravel into the soil or make natural and attractive supports from branches. It's important to insert them fairly early so that the shoots grow up straight without breaking.

➤ **Sterile blooms**
Flowers whose reproductive organs have been stunted or transformed, for example, into flower petals (as with many double blooms). Consequently, they cannot be fertilized and propagated through seeds. The blooms

can thus be kept for a particularly long time.

➤ True to kind or pure
A plant that matches the description of the variety. Generative propagation does not always produce offspring that are true to kind, with the same characteristics as the parent plants.

➤ Variety
Term used to designate the specific propagation of a species. The variety name is appended to the genus and species name. It is written with a capital letter, but not in italics, and is placed in single quotation marks.

➤ Vegetative propagation
The means by which cuttings, dividing, runners, or shoots are used for propagation to produce young plants that are totally identical to the mother plant.

➤ Species
The second part of the botanical name indicates the variety and distinguishes the various members of a →genus. *Papaver orientale* belongs to the genus of poppies—*Papaver*. It's the name of the variety—*orientale*— that clarifies which poppy is meant, namely the Turkish poppy. The species name is always written with a small first letter and in italics.

➤ Well-drained soil
Soil in which the water is naturally removed. In the garden, this generally becomes necessary only when nothing will grow in extremely wet, heavy, compacted soils, or with plants that thrive only in very porous locations. This can be done by providing a light layer of gravel at root level.

Plant Portraits

For perennials, summer flowers, and bulb plants, the following portraits will help you quickly find the plants you are looking for! Plunge into the flowering multitude and draw inspiration for some new plantings!

Finding What You Need

The garden flowers are arranged in the following groups in the portrait section:

➤ **Perennials:** primarily winter-hardy perennials for sunny to shaded flowerbeds; typical rock garden plants and mat-forming perennials are not included.

➤ **Annuals and biennials:** the most important spring and summer flowers for flowerbeds.

➤ **Bulb and tuber plants:** winter-hardy and frost-sensitive species for all locations and seasons.

Within the individual groups, the flowers are arranged alphabetically according to their botanical names. You can use the index to find the English name of any given plant.

The Plant Portraits

You will see an overview of the most important information next to the photos: the height and flowering time of each plant. The symbols quickly indicate the correct location, usage, and special features such as fragrance and toxicity. The current botanical names are sometimes not very familiar. The old names still crop up even in nurseries and catalogs. These, along with other names used in English, are listed in the "Also Known as" category. The remaining categories contain the following information:

Family: The botanical and English family names.

Native to: The countries or regions in which the plant species is naturally found. This information is left out in the case of special strains.

Bloom: The precise appearance of the bloom.

Appearance: Everything concerning the plant's growth, its leaves, and its stature. There is also information about spreading.

Location: Data on the light and soil conditions the plant prefers.

Planting: Recommendations on preferred or required planting times for perennials, and bulb and tuber plants; also the times for planting and starting seeds for annuals and biennials.

Care: The most important information on watering, cutting, supporting, and providing winter protection.
Arrangement: Appropriate companion plants and more about how the plants can be used in the flowerbed.
Notes: Information about toxicity of plants, their fragrance, or when the plants should be cut for the vase.
Species/Variety: The most important relatives or similar species and varieties.

The Symbols Used

 The plant is particularly undemanding and is a good choice even for beginners. (Note requirements for location and care.)

 The location should be bright and sunny for the greater part of the day.

 The location should not be in the sun, especially at midday.

 The location should not be in the sun.

 Fairly sandy, porous, continually moderately dry to dry soil.

 Fairly loamy, porous, moderately dry to moist soil.

 Fairly loamy or clayey, continually moist to damp soil.

 The plant is suited to being planted by itself or in groups of up to three plants.

 Should be planted in fairly small groups of three to seven plants.

 Plants for fairly large groups or ground cover; with bulb plants, also a tendency to run wild

 The flowers are appropriate for a vase or for drying.

 Parts of the plant have an aromatic fragrance.

 The plant is poisonous or irritating to the skin.

Perennials
from A to Z

Perennials dazzle with their sumptuous
flowers and come up every year—and in
many shapes and varieties. Each one has
its own life cycle: even if individual species
flower for only a short while, the times
during which the panicles, umbels, and
tapestry of flowers appear fill nearly the
entire year.

Height:
*28–47 inches/
70–120 cm*
Blooming Time:
June–Sept./Oct.

Achillea filipendulina

Fernleaf Yarrow ✿
Also Known as: Cloth of Gold

Family: Compositae (*Asteraceae*)
Native to: Turkey, Caucasus, Iran, Afghanistan, Central Asia
Bloom: Flat, dish-like umbels in various shades of yellow
Appearance: Fir upright, solid clusters with filigree, some-
times gray-green feathery leaves
Location: Undemanding; prefers full sun and warmth
Planting: Can be planted from March through October
Care: Undemanding; in the spring cut off faded blooms, since
the stands of stalks are attractive even in winter.
Arrangement: Tall varieties are appropriate for the rear of the
flowerbed; shorter ones can be placed more toward the front.
Blue perennials such as *Delphinium, Echinops, Geranium,
Nepeta, and Salvia* as well as yellow and red flowers (e.g.,
Helenium) are good companions.
Notes: Cutting flower, good for drying; pungent fragrance
Species/Varieties: Coronation Gold (32 in./80 cm, yellow,
silver-gray leaves, → illus.), Parker's Variety (39–47 in./
100–120 cm, golden yellow), Credo (32 in./80
cm, lemon yellow)

Height:
*24–31.5 inches/
60–80 cm*
Blooming Time:
June–Aug.

Achillea millefolium

Common Yarrow ❀
Also known as: Milfoil

Family: Compositae (*Asteraceae*)
Native to: Europe, Central Asia, North America, Australia
Bloom: Flat umbels in red, pink, orange, copper, and white
Appearance: Fine feathery leaves; readily sends out runners
Location: Undemanding; preferably full sun; porous soil
Planting: Self-seeding in appropriate locations
Care: Regular pruning encourages new blooms.
Arrangement: The species is suited for natural appearing beds
and is attractive with varieties that produce blue flowers, such
as *Erigeron, Gypsophila, Salvia, and Scabiosa,* and medium-tall
grasses such as *Panicum* and *Stipa.*
Species/Varieties: Lilac Beauty (20 in./50 cm, purplish pink),
Paprika (20 in./50 cm, brick red), Schneetaler (27.5 in./70 cm,
pure white), Summerwine (28 in./70 cm, wine red), Terra-
cotta (24 in./60 cm, reddish brown), Walter Funcke (20 in./50
cm, orange-red, gray foliage), Sumpf-Schafgarbe, *A. ptarmica*
Snowball (12–28 in./30–70 cm, double, white flowers)

Height:
*36–59 inches/
90–150 cm*
**Blooming
Time:**
Sept.–Oct.

Aconitum carmichaelii Arendsii Group

Monkshood
Also known as: Autumn Flowering Monkshood

Family: Buttercup or Crowfoot plants (*Ranunculaceae*)
Bloom: Panicles with helmet-shaped individual flowers
Appearance: Magnificent clusters; strong, sturdy, upright
stems; large, incised, leathery leaves that are shiny on top
Location: Moist, rich soils; preferably with lightly wooded
border; however, also tolerates sun and shade
Planting: Propagation through dividing or seeding
Care: Autumn flowering varieties can winter over.
Arrangement: Appropriate in all colors; attractive with
Anemone hupehensis, Aruncus, Astilbe, Cimicifuga, Thalictrum
Notes: All parts contain the strong toxin aconitine.
Species/Varieties: *A. × cammarum* Bicolor (47 in./120 cm,
blue with white); *A. carmichaelii* Wilsonii group (59 in./
150 cm, medium blue, also in white); *A. napellus* (blooms
earlier: June/July–Aug., 32–47 in./80–120 cm, blue-purple),
Newry Blue (47 in./120 cm, dark blue); *A. lycoctonus* ssp.
neapolitanum (39 in./100 cm, light yellow, June/July)

Height:
*31–35 inches/
80–90 cm*
**Blooming
Time:**
July–Aug.

Agastache foeniculum

Anise hyssop
Also known as: Blue Giant Hyssop

Family: Mint plants (*Lamiaceae*)
Native to: USA, Mexico
Bloom: Long panicles; in thick whorls, short lips on calyces
Appearance: Bushy growth; attractive nettle-like leaves, ovate and with short tips; dark green top and shiny, hairy, nearly white underside
Location: Sun to partial shade; porous and moderately dry
Planting: Preferably in late spring
Care: Winter protection is recommended in cold areas.
Arrangement: *Achillea, Anthemis, Echinacea, Eryngium, Geranium, Knautia, Monarda,* and *Solidago* are a good match.
Notes: The entire plant has a fragrance of anise or fennel.
Species/Varieties: Golden Jubilee (yellow leaves); *A. rugosa* (24 in./60 cm, pinkish red, completely winter hardy), Alba (white); *Agastache* Blue Fortune (35 in./90 cm, purple-blue, → illus.); *A. barberi* (60) cm, Firebird (salmon colored), Pink Panther (purple)

Height:
*12–16 inches/
30–40 cm*
**Blooming
Time:**
June–Aug.

Alchemilla mollis

Lady's Mantle ✿

Family: Rose plants *(Rosaceae)*
Native to: Caucasus, Iran, Russia
Bloom: Yellow-green, veil-like clusters of flowers
Appearance: Bushy growth; dew and water droplets collect on the leaves; summer-green rosettes
Location: Very undemanding; thrives even in dry shade; quite resistant to drought; very competitive
Planting: Can be planted from March through October
Care: Cutting back significantly after the first flowering in June encourages new flowering; the plant sprouts anew.
Arrangement: Fits in with nearly all perennials and in all plantings, also suited for flowerbed border; attractive varieties for that purpose are *Astilbe, Brunnera, Campanula, Euphorbia, Geranium × magnificum, Geum, Heughera, Hosta,* and *Nepeta*
Species/Varieties: *A. epipsila* (8 in./20 cm, green-yellow, June–Aug.) *A. erythropoda* (4–6 in. /10–15 cm, green-yellow, June–July, not robust); *A. alpina* (2 in./5 cm, cream-color, gleaming silver leaves, attractive in rock gardens)

Height:
*8–20 inches/
20–50 cm*
**Blooming
Time:**
July–Sept.

Anaphalis triplinervis

Pearly Everlasting ✿

Family: Compositae *(Asteraceae)*
Native to: Himalayas
Bloom: Small, white, strawflower-like blooms in small umbels
Appearance: Bushy plant; leafy stem; gray or white wooly leaves; does not grow profusely
Location: Sunny and warm, also tolerates hot locations; on preferably dry, porous, sandy soils with low nutrient content
Planting: Can be planted from March through October
Care: Easy to care for; if necessary, fertilize with care
Arrangement: Goes with low *Anthemis, Aster* (e.g., *Aster dumosus*), *Campanula, Centranthus, Lavandula, Liatris, Nepeta, Salvia,* and *Sedum telephium;* also in foreground of flowerbed
Notes: Good for cutting and drying
Species/Varieties: Summer Snow (compact, → illus.), Silberregen; *A. margaritaceae* (20–24 in./50–60 cm, white, gray hairy leaf, propagates through runners, Neuschnee and Schwefellicht varieties (also marketed as *Helichrysum*, sulfur yellow)

Height:
*35–47 inches/
90–120 cm*
**Blooming
Time:**
June–Aug.

Anchusa azurea

Italian Bugloss
Also known as: Italian Alkanet, Loddon Royalist

Family: Borage plants *(Boraginaceae)*
Native to: Europe, Caucasus, Central Asia, Northern Africa
Bloom: Small blue bundle of flowers on branched stems
Appearance: Erect growth; with hairy, rough, fairly long ovate leaves; often quite short-lived
Location: Sun; porous soils rich in humus; quite sensitive to winter dampness
Planting: Plant in the spring.
Care: Cut back after flowering to strengthen plants for the winter; in addition, cover plants.
Arrangement: Leaves empty spots after flowering; goes well with *Achillea, Buphtalmum, Centaurea, Inula,* and *Oenothera*
Notes: Flowers are good for cutting.
Species/Varieties: Loddon Royalist (gleaming blue, → illus.), Dropmore (up to 59 in./150 cm, gentian blue), Feltham Pride Strain (35 in./90 cm, gentian blue), Little John (24 in./60 cm, dark blue), Pride of Dover (azure blue)

Height:
*28–39 inches/
70–100 cm*
Blooming Time:
Aug./Sept.–Oct.

Anemone hupehensis var. *japonica*

Japanese Anemone

Family: Buttercup or Crowfoot plants (*Ranunculaceae*)
Native to: Japan, China
Bloom: Single, semidouble, or double bowl-shaped flowers in white, several shades of pink, and red
Appearance: Large leaf clusters; the erect flower stems jut out; base leaves on stem; new plants arise from the roots
Location: Partial shade, with nutrient-rich, moist soil
Planting: Prefers spring planting
Care: In exposed locations, cover for winter (e.g., with gravel); fertilize occasionally
Arrangement: Attractive with white, pink, red, and blue, for example, with *Aconitum, Aster ericoides, A. cordifolius, Astilbe,* and *Cimicifuga*
Species/Varieties: Ouverture (light pink, → illus.), Queen Charlotte (pink, semidouble), Rosenschale (pink, red rim), Honorine Jobert (white), Whirlwind (white, semidouble); *A. hupehensis* var. *huphensis* Hadspen Abundance (dark pink); *A. tomentosa* Rubustissima (pink, lush growth)

Height:
*16–24 inches/
40–60 cm*
**Blooming
Time:**
May–Sept.

Anthemis tinctoria

Golden Marguerite
Also Known as: Yellow Chamomile, Ox-eye Chamomile

Family: Compositae *(Asteraceae)*
Native to: Europe, Turkey, Syria, Caucasus, Iran
Bloom: Daisy flowers in various shades of yellow
Appearance: Bushy, clustered growth; feathery leaves with green tops and more or less gray, hairy undersides
Location: Sunny, warm; porous, fairly sandy soils
Planting: Preferably in late spring
Care: Cut back in the fall to give the plants strength for the winter; cover in cold locations.
Arrangement: An attractive eyecatcher until cutting back; goes with *Aster, Centranthus, Erigeron, Knautia, Nepeta,* and *Salvia*
Notes: The more flowers you cut off, the more new buds form. The plant has an aromatic fragrance.
Species/Varieties: Beauty of Grallagh (golden yellow), E. C. Buxton (lemon yellow), Kelwayi (lemon yellow), Wargrave (cream-yellow); *A. marschalliana* (10 in./25 cm, golden yellow, silvery leaves); *Chamaemelum nobile* Plena (4–10 in./ 10–25 cm, double, small white blooms, June–Oct., fine green leaves)

35

Height:
*12–28 inches/
30–70 cm*
**Blooming
Time:**
May–June

Aquilegia caerulea

Rocky Mountain Columbine ✿

Family: Buttercup or Crowfoot plants (*Ranunculaceae*)
Native to: USA
Bloom: Spurred flowers in white, pink, red, blue; also bicolor;
single and double; multiple bloomer
Appearance: Finely haired stalk; basal, bluish frosted leaves
from which the sturdy flower stems project upward
Location: Sun to partial shade; soil high in humus and moist
Planting: Self-seeding in appropriate locations
Care: Very undemanding
Arrangement: Good for nostalgic flowerbeds (e.g., with
Alchemilla, tall *Camanula, Dicentra, Digitalis,* and *Primula*)
Species/Varieties: Crimson Star (red with white, → illus.),
Blue Star (blue with white), Crystal (white); McKana hybrids
(large flowering mixture, 20–24 in./50–60 cm); Alpine
Columbine, *A. alpina* (16 in./40 cm, blue); Golden
Columbine, *A. chrysantha* Yellow Queen (24–31 in./60–80 cm,
yellow); Swarf Fan Columbine, *A. flabellata* 6–10 in./15–25
cm, various colors); Winky Double Red White (20 in./50 cm,
double, red and white)

Height:
*28 inches/
70 cm*
**Blooming
Time:**
Aug.–Sept.

Artemisia ludoviciana 'Silver Queen'

Mugwort
Also Known as: White Sage

Family: Compositae *(Asteraceae)*
Native to: North America
Bloom: Inconspicuous and small, pale yellow in tight panicles
Appearance: Silver-gray, lanceolate, incised leaves, hairy, white undersides, nearly glabrous top when mature; lush growth
Location: Sunny, warm; porous, fairly dry soils
Planting: Can be planted from March through October
Care: Restrain excessive growth by trimming.
Arrangement: Good in white gardens, but also with dark flowers and leaves, such as *Achillea millefolium, Aster, Heuchera, Knautia, Platycodon, Salvia,* and *Sedum* Matrona
Notes: The leaves of most varieties have an aromatic fragrance.
Species/Varieties: The genus includes aromatic herbs and showy species. Dusty Miller Sagewort, *A. stelleriana* (8–16 in./20–40 cm, hairy white leaf), Lambrook Silver (28 in./70 cm, gray-green, finely incised leaf), Powis Castle (20 in./50 cm, fine silvery leaves, woody); *A. lactiflora* Guizho group (71 in./180 cm, cream-white, arched panicles, Aug.–Sept.)

Height:
*59–79 inches/
150–200 cm*
**Blooming
Time:**
June–July

Aruncus dioicus

Goat's Beard ✿

Family: Rose plants *(Rosaceae)*
Native to: Europe, Caucasus
Bloom: Large, cream-white panicles of flowers
Appearance: Magnificent clusters with green feathery leaves that give rise to the blooms
Location: Shady and cool; preferably in moist ground
Planting: Can be planted from March through October
Care: Very easy to care for
Arrangement: Attractive specimen plant for shaded flowerbeds; goes well with *Campanula latifolia, Astilbe, Digitalis,* and *Rodgersia*
Notes: There are male and female plants that are distinguished by pure white or yellowish flowers. If both are present, they seed themselves abundantly. Slightly poisonous.
Species/Varieties: Small Goat's Beard, *A. aethusiflius* (12 in./30 cm, white, fern-like leaves, orange color in the fall) *A. sinensis,* Zweiweltenkind (59–71 in./150–180 cm, cream-white, brown shoots, tolerates a little more dryness); *Aruncus* hybrid: Horatio (32 in./80 cm, turns colors in the fall)

Height:
31–39 inches/ 80–100 cm
Blooming Time:
May–June

Asphodeline lutea

Jacob's Rod
Also Known as: King's Spear, Yellow Asphodel

Family: Asphodel plants *(Asphodelaceae)*
Native to: Alps, Balkans, Caucasus
Bloom: Thick clusters of yellow flowers with individual flowers up to an inch/3 cm or more; late-blooming attractive multiple fruits into the fall
Appearance: Leek-like, linear leaves; remains green in winter and grows both in a rosette close to the ground and on the secure flower stalk; bluish green leaves; sends out short runners
Location: Full sun and warm; dry, porous soil that's neither meager nor poor in nutrients
Planting: Prefers to remain in one place for many years
Care: Cover for the winter in cold areas
Arrangement: Large and attractive because of the early blooms, the fruits, and the leaves. The overall shape goes well with compact plants such as *Bergenia, Dianthus, Kniphofia, Lavandula, Nepeta, Origanum,* and *Sedum.*
Species/Varieties: Yellow Candle (24 in./60 cm, yellow, green berries); *A. liburnica* (43 in./100 cm, yellow, night bloomer, June–July)

Height:
*16–24 inches/
40–60 cm*
**Blooming
Time:**
July–Sept.

Aster amellus

Italian Aster
Also Known as: European Michelmas Daisy

Family: Compositae *(Asteraceae)*
Native to: Europe, Caucasus
Bloom: Daisy blooms in blue, purple, shades of pink, and white
Appearance: Coarsely haired, lanceolate leaves on branched stems; not always sturdy
Location: Sunny, warm; porous soils containing lime; dampness in winter creates lots of problems for the plants
Planting: Best to plant in the spring
Care: Provide support if needed
Arrangement: Mix varieties or with *Achillea, Anaphalis, Coreopsis, Echinacea, Rudbeckia,* and grasses
Notes: Cut blooms for vase.
Species/Varieties: Veilchenkönigen (dark purple, → illus.), Hermann Löns (lavender-blue, large flowers), Lady Hindlip (pink), Silbersee (light blue); *A. × frikartii:* varieties: Monk (32 in./80 cm, light blue), Wunder von Stäfa (32 in./80 cm, lavender blue); *A. pyrenaeus* Lutetia (20 in./50 cm, soft purple, low-lying shoots)

Height:
*8–18 inches/
20–45 cm*
**Blooming
Time:**
Aug.–Oct.

Aster dumosus

Bushy Aster

Family: Compositae *(Asteraceae)*
Native to: Eastern Canada, USA
Bloom: Daisy flowers in white, pink, red, blue, violet; single, semidouble, and double
Appearance: Thick, bushy, compact plants with smooth, dark green lanceolate leaves; amply branched
Location: Sun or partial shade; moist to damp soils
Planting: Best planted in the spring
Care: Older plants are subject to mildew in unfavorable weather conditions; if that occurs, take in and divide plants.
Arrangement: Even before flowering, these plants look very attractive and thus are very good for planting borders.
Species/Varieties: Silver Carpet (silver-gray, → illus.), Kristina (white, semidouble), Blue Lagoon (dark blue), Heinz Richard (pink), Jenny (purple-red, double); similar: *A. sedifolius* Nanus (16 in./40 cm, light blue, star-shaped flowers); *A. pansus* Snowflurry (8 in., small white blooms, low-lying shoots)

41

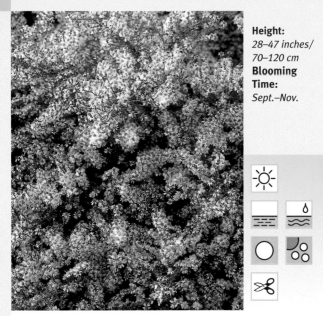

Height:
*28–47 inches/
70–120 cm*
**Blooming
Time:**
Sept.–Nov.

Aster ericoides
Heath Aster

Family: Compositae (*Asteraceae)*
Native to: Canada, USA, Mexico
Bloom: Small daisy flowers in white, pink, soft blue
Appearance: Long, fine-leafed shoots; quite sturdy
Location: Sun; soil rich in nutrients and not too dry
Planting: Best planted in the spring
Care: Water in severe drought; provide support if necessary.
Arrangement: Wild character, plant with Bushgrass and Switchgrass, and with *Eupatorium, Physostegia,* and *Sedum.*
Species/Varieties: Blue Star (blue), Erlkönig (light violet), Esther (pink), Snow Fir (white); similar: *A. pringlei*, Monte Cassino (39–47 in./100–120 cm, white, Sept.–Nov.); Blue Forest Aster, *A. cordifolius* (28–47 in./70–120 cm, Sept., varieties in shades of blue); *A. vinculus* Lovely (28 in./70 cm, pink, Oct.–Nov.); *A. laevis* (51 in./130 cm, lavender-blue, Aug.–Sept.; *A. lateriflorus* 24–39 in./60–100 cm, pink-white, Aug.–Sept., erect bushes), Horizontalis (24 in./60 cm, white, dark leaves); *A. trinervius* ssp. *microcephalus* Asran (24 in./60 cm, pink)

Height:
*16–28 inches/
40–70 cm*
**Blooming
Time:**
July–Sept.

Aster linosyris

Goldilocks ✿

Family: Compositae *(Asteraceae)*
Native to: Europe, Turkey, Caucasus, Algeria
Bloom: Small, golden yellow flower heads; in contrast to other asters, they consist not of ligulate flowers, but rather exclusively of tubular flowers
Appearance: Bushy plant, sometimes spreading out widely; fine, needle-like leaves on erect, unbranched stems
Location: Sun; preferably dry, loamy, sandy soils; also tolerates windy locations
Planting: Prefers spring planting
Care: If leaves turn yellow, cut them off.
Arrangement: Goes well with *Aster amellus, Coreopsis verticillata,* small flowering *Hemerocallis, Linum perenne,* and *Silene viscaria*
Notes: The blooms are well suited to cutting.
Species/Varieties: Similar: Solidaster, × *Solidaster luteus* (24 in./60 cm, tiny, light yellow aster flowers in tight clusters, July–Sept., Lemore variety)

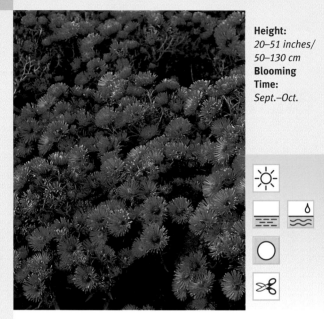

Height:
*20–51 inches/
50–130 cm*
**Blooming
Time:**
Sept.–Oct.

Aster novae-angliae

New England Aster
Also Known as: Michaelmas Daisy

Family: Compositae *(Asteraceae)*
Native to: USA, Central Europe
Bloom: Single, white, pink, red, and blue daisy flowers
Appearance: Large, solid, healthy bushes that are leafless toward the top; rough, lanceolate leaves, branched stems
Location: Sun; moist to damp soils rich in nutrients; in sandy ground, sensitive to summer drought
Planting: Best planted in spring
Care: With varieties that aren't sturdy, cut back to half at the beginning of July; this also retards flowering
Arrangement: Good partners include *Helenium, Heliopsis, Leucanthemella, Phlox,* and *Solidago;* short perennials such as *Nepeta* and *Sedum* help hide the lower third of the bare stems
Notes: Most varieties close their flowers at night
Species/Varieties: Alma Pötschke (pink, → illus.), Barr's Blue (deep blue), Herbstschnee (white), Purple Dome (24 in./60 cm, violet), Rubinschatz (ruby red), Violetta (dark purple)

Height:
*20–47 inches/
50–120 cm*
**Blooming
Time:**
Aug.–Oct.

Aster novi-belgii

New York Aster
Also Known as: Michaelmas Daisy

Family: Compositae *(Asteraceae)*
Native to: Canada, USA, Europe
Bloom: Blue, pink, and white daisy flowers in clusters; single, semidouble, and double
Appearance: Erect, branched shoots; smooth leaves, thinning toward the top; not always sturdy
Location: Sunny; soil containing lime, nutrient; moist
Planting: Best planted in the spring
Care: Smooth-leafed asters can be susceptible to mildew; it's preferable to transplant, fertilize, and water them occasionally during drought; cut back varieties that aren't sturdy by half at the beginning of June
Arrangement: See *Aster novae-angliae*
Species/Varieties: Sailor Boy (dark blue, semidouble, → illus.). Schöne von Dietlikon (dark blue), Marie Ballard (light blue, double), Bonningdale White (white, semidouble), Crimson Brocade (carmine), Royal Ruby (20 in./50 cm, red, semidouble), Fellowship (light pink, double); *A. divaricatus* (24–32 in./60–80 cm, small, white flowers)

45

Height:
*24–39 inches/
60–100 cm*
**Blooming
Time:**
June–Aug.

Astilbe × arendsii

Astilbe
Also Known as: Bridal Veil, Bessingham Beauty

Family: Saxifrage plants *(Saxifragaceae)*
Bloom: Thick, erect, partially overhanging panicles in glowing red, pink, purple, and white
Appearance: Erect, bushy growth; feathery leaves
Location: Partial to full shade; moist to damp ground; tolerates more sun in damp ground
Planting: Best if set out in springtime
Care: The plants continually work their way upward in the earth, so keep adding soil. Divide clusters every few years.
Arrangement: Luminous flowers in shady areas; combine red varieties with more subdued colors, for example, with *Anemone hupehensis, Alchemilla, Bergenia,* and *Cimicifuga*
Notes: Blooms are good for cutting.
Species/Varieties: Anita Pfeiffer (28 in./70 cm, salmon color), Brautschleier (32 in., 80 cm, white, overhanging flowers), Cattleya (40 in./100 cm, pink), Diamond (36 in./90 cm, white), Fanal (24 in./60 cm, red, dark shoots)

Height:
*20 inches/
50 cm*
**Blooming
Time:**
June–July

Astilbe japonica

Florist's Spirea
Also Known as: Japanese Astilbe

Family: Saxifrage plants *(Saxifragaceae)*
Native to: Japan
Bloom: Small, pyramid-shaped panicles in white, pink, and red
Appearance: Erect plant; feathery, summer-green foliage
Location: Partial to full shade; moist to damp ground; the
damper the location, the more sun the plant tolerates
Planting: Best planted in the spring
Care: Add soil if plants work themselves upward.
Arrangement: Attractive with *Bergenia* × *Heucherella, Hosta,
Tiarella,* and shade grasses such as *Carex morrowii*
Notes: Blooms are good for cutting.
Species/Varieties: Germany (white), Europe (light pink),
Mainz (purple-pink), Köln (dark red); Japanese Astilbe, *A.
simplicifolia* (12–20 in./30–50 cm, white, pink, or red, loose
overhanging flower panicles), Alba (white), Aphrodite (red),
Praecox (pink) Chinese Astilbe, *A. chinensis* var. *pumila*
(10 in./25 cm, erect, pink blooms, good for ground cover)

Height:
*35–51 inches/
90–130 cm*
**Blooming
Time:**
July–Aug.

Astilbe thunbergii

Thunberg's Astilbe

Family: Saxifrage plants *(Saxifragaceae)*
Bloom: Mostly overhanging, fragrant flower panicles in white, pink, purple-pink, and red
Appearance: Erect, loose, bushy growth; feathery, summer-green leaves
Location: Partial to full shade; damp to moist soils; tolerates more sun in moist ground
Planting: Best to set out in the spring
Care: Add soil if the clusters work their way out of the soil.
Arrangement: Attractive with *Aconitum, Astrantia, Campanula, Cimicifuga, Digitalis, Geranium, Hemerocallis,* and *Hosta*
Species/Varieties: Ostrich Plume (39 in./100 cm, salmon color, → illus.), Jo Ophorst (35 in./90 cm, dark pink-purple, erect panicles), Moerheimii (47 in./120 cm, white), Red Charm (35 in./90 cm, luminous red); similar to Chinese Astilbe/False Spirea/False Goat's beard, *A. chinensis* var. *taquetii* (39 in./100 cm, purple-red, erect, tolerates slightly more dryness than other varieties)

Height:
*20–28 inches/
50–70 cm*
**Blooming
Time:**
July–Sept.

Astrantia major ssp. *major*

Astrantia Major

Family: Umbellliferae *(Apiaceae)*
Native to: Europe
Bloom: Grayish white, pink, and red, sheathed leaves surround the real, inconspicuous flowers located in umbels
Appearance: Hand-shaped partly variegated leaves that give rise to the erect flower stems
Location: Sun to shade; moist to moderately damp, porous soils with a fair amount of nutrients
Planting: Prefers spring planting
Care: Water during persistent drought.
Arrangement: The red varieties are attractive with red-leafed plants such as *Heuchera* and the white with variegated *Hosta*. Also good with *Alchemilla, Anemone, Astilbe,* and *Trollius*
Species/Varieties: Rosea (pink, → illus.), Rose Symphony (pink-red), Claret (dark red), Ruby Wedding (dark red, dark stems), Hadspen Blood (almost black), Shaggy (= Margery Fish, twisted, white, sheathed leaves), Sunningdale Variegated (pink, yellow variegated leaves that turn green in the summer)

49

Height:
*10–24 inches/
25–60 cm*
**Blooming
Time:**
March–May

Bergenia Hybrids

Bergenia ✤

Family: Saxifrage plants *(Saxigragaceae)*
Bloom: White, pink, red, purple small bells in loose umbels
Appearance: The large, stout, leathery leaves remain considerably lower than the flowers. Many varieties turn reddish in the fall. All are wintergreen.
Location: Sun to shade; practically any type of soil
Planting: Can be planted from spring through the fall
Care: Appreciates regular additions of compost. If you want to rejuvenate the plants or keep them particularly compact, cut them off at ground level every couple of years after flowering.
Arrangement: Fits into the widest variety of locations. With their year-round attractive appearance and striking structure, they are perfect for edging a bed or as focus point in the flowerbed
Notes: Positively resistant to slugs
Species/Varieties: Abendglocken or Evening Bells (dark red), Bergenia Morning Red (pink, late bloomer), Opal (purple-pink), Purple Bells (purple-red, always blooms late), or Silver Light'(white-pink, fragrant); Altai Bergenia, *B. cordifolia* (12–16 in./30–40 cm, violet, pink, April–May)

Height:
*32–47 inches/
80–120 cm*
**Blooming
Time:**
June–Oct.

Bistorta amplexicaulis

Bistorta amplexicaulis
Also Known as: Mountain Fleece

Family: Knotweed plants *(Polygonaceae)*
Native to: Himalayas
Bloom: Small, white, pink, and red flowers in thick heads
Appearance: Loose, bushy growth; lanceolate leaves that completely surround the stem
Location: Sun to partial shade; prefers damp ground
Planting: Can be planted from spring to fall
Care: Water during fairly prolonged drought
Arrangement: Long, attractive; the candle-shaped flowers go well with umbellates, panicle flowers, or compositae, for example with *Anemone hupehensis, Astrantia, Campanula, Echinacea, Eupatorium, Phlox, Scabiosa, Thalictrum, Veronicastrum,* and grasses
Species/Varieties: Roseum (dark pink, → illus.), Atropurpureum (dark red), Firetail (= Speciosum, scarlet), Summer Dance (pink), Album (white), *B. officinalis.* High Tatra (32 in./80 cm, red, June–Aug.), Superbum (24 in./60 cm, pink, May–June)

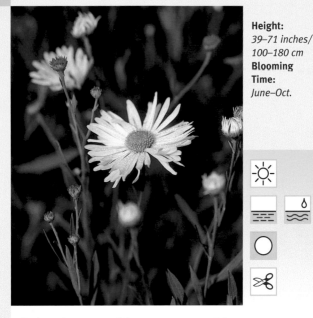

Height:
*39–71 inches/
100–180 cm*
**Blooming
Time:**
June–Oct.

Boltonia asteroides var. *asteroides*

White Doll's Daisy ✿

Family: Compositae *(Asteraceae)*
Native to: USA
Bloom: Small, pink and white clouds of flowers similar to asters
Appearance: Lush clusters with smooth, partially gray, frosted, lanceolate leaves; not always sturdy
Location: Sunny and warm; in moist to damp soil rich in nutrients
Planting: Best planted in the spring
Care: Support varieties that are inclined to fall over.
Arrangement: Goes well in natural-looking plantings (e.g., with *Cosmos bipinnatus, Phlox maculata, Solidago,* and *Veronicastrum*) ideally, support with adjacent plants (e.g., with *Helenium* and *Rudbeckia*)
Notes: The flowers are very good for cutting.
Species/Varieties: Pink Beauty (39 in./100 cm, soft pink, loose overhanging shoots, sturdy), Snowbank (47 in./120 cm, white, sturdy); *B. asteroids* var. *latisquama* (71 in./180 cm, white), Nana (28 in./70 cm, pink-purple)

Height:
*12–15 inches/
30–50 cm*
**Blooming
Time:**
April–May

Brunnera macrophylla

Siberian Bugloss ❀

Family: Borage plants *(Boraginaceae)*
Native to: Caucasus, Western Siberia
Bloom: Small blue flowers in small, loose, branched clusters
Appearance: Bushy, clustered growth; large, rough, heart-shaped leaves, partly variegated or containing light spots
Location: Preferably partial shade and not too dry; however, also withstands deep shade and full sun
Planting: *Brunnera* seeds itself in damp locations
Care: Water during fairly extended drought
Arrangement: Although it blooms early, the plant still remains attractive later on, so it should not be planted in the back of the flowerbed. Appropriate neighbors include *Alchemilla, Astilbe, Dicentra, Doronicum, Epimedium, Primula,* and *Trollius.*
Notes: The plant often produces an abundance of seeds.
Species/Varieties: Betty Bovering (white), Hadspen Cream (blue flowers, green leaves with irregular, light edge), Langtrees (blue flowers, silvery spotted foliage), Variegata (blue flowers, white mottled leaves)

Height:
*16–24 inches/
40–60 cm*
**Blooming
Time:**
June–Sept.

Buphtalmum salicifolium

Yellow Oxeye Daisy ✿
Also Known as: Alpengold

Family: Compositae *(Asteraceae)*
Native to: Eastern and Central Europe
Bloom: Yellow daisy flowers
Appearance: Thick, sturdy, bushy clusters with small, lanceolate leaves
Location: Sun; the soil should be porous, moderately dry, and not too rich in nutrients; likes lime
Planting: Can be planted from the spring through the fall.
Care: Cut back significantly in the fall.
Arrangement: Good contrast to blue flowers (e.g., *Aster, Nepeta, Pseudolysimachion,* and *Salvia*); harmonizes with red (e.g., *Centranthus, Erigeron,* and *Helenium*)
Notes: The blooms hold up well in a vase.
Species/Varieties: Alpengold (20 in./50 cm, golden yellow), Dora (16 in./40 cm, orange yellow, → illus.); similar, but much larger: *Telekia speciosa* (47 in./120 cm, yellow, June–Aug., sun to partial shade, moist soil, seeds itself in suitable locations)

Height:
15–20 inches/
30–50 cm
Blooming Time:
Aug.–Oct.

Calamintha nepeta ssp. *nepeta*

Lesser Calamint ✿

Family: Mint plants *(Lamiaceae)*
Native to: Europe
Bloom: Small blue or white flowers in loose cymes
Appearance: Compact growth, sometimes a bit woody; small, rounded to ovate leaves on erect stems
Location: Preferably sunny and warm; fairly dry, porous soil; however, it also thrives in moist ground and in partial shade
Planting: Can be planted from spring through fall
Care: Cut back (only moderately) in the spring
Arrangement: Attractive in a natural setting; suitable partners are *Aster amellus, Anaphalis, Bergenia, Coreopsis, Gypsophila, Salvia, Saponaria, Sedum, Sidalcea,* and *Stachys byzantina*
Notes: Flowers and leaves smell like mint.
Species/Varieties: Blue Cloud (16 in./40 cm, larger, violet-blue flowers), White Cloud (12 in./30 cm, white); Large-flowered Calamint, *C. grandiflora* (12–16 in./30–40 cm, purple-pink, July–Sept.) Gottfried Kuhn (often listed as *C. nepeta* varieties, 16 in./40 cm, purple-pink), Variegata (pink, yellow variegated foliage)

Height:
*8–20 inches/
20–50 cm*
**Blooming
Time:**
June–July

Campanula glomerata

Clustered Bellflower

Family: Bellflower plants *(Campanulaceae)*
Native to: Europe, Siberia, Central Asia
Bloom: Large, blue and white bellflowers that perch like thick bundles in the uppermost leaf axils
Appearance: Erect growth with powerful stalks; toothed, wide, lanceolate, rough leaves; grows runners
Location: Sun to partial shade; withstands short drought in porous soils; likes lime
Planting: Can be planted from spring through fall
Care: Cut back after blooms have gone by to stimulate formation of new shoots; water during periods of dryness
Arrangement: Appropriate to nearly all flower colors; attractive partners include *Achillea, Alchemilla, Coreopsis,* and *Phlox*
Species/Varieties: Acaulis (8 in./20 cm, blue-violet), Alba (12 in./30 cm, white), Dahurica (20 in./50 cm, dark blue), Joan Elliot (16–20 in./40–50 cm, dark blue); Milky Bellflower, *C. lactiflora* (31–39 in./80–100 cm, July–Sept.), Alba (white), Loddon Anne (pink), Prichard's Variety (violet), Superba (dark blue)

Height:
*35–39 inches/
90–100 cm*
**Blooming
Time:**
June–July

Campanula latifolia

Giant Bellflower
Also Known as: Great Bellflower

Family: Bellflower plants *(Campanulaceae)*
Native to: Europe, Caucasus, Central Asia, Himalayas, Turkey
Bloom: Large, pendent blue-violet or white flowers
Appearance: Narrow, erect growth; sturdy, upright flower stalks; long, pointed, rough leaves
Location: For shady to half- or lightly shaded areas in normal garden plots; also appropriate for new flowerbeds
Planting: Can be planted from spring through fall
Care: Provide support if necessary; water during drought
Arrangement: Appropriate neighbors include *Aconitum, Anemone hupehensis, Astilbe, Astrantia, Cimicifuge,* and *Digitalis*
Notes: Good for cutting; susceptible to snails and slugs
Species/Varieties: Alba (white), Macrantha (dark violet), Macrantha Alba (white); similar: *C. trachelium* (32 in./80 cm, violet blue, June–July) Album (white); *Campanula* hybrid varieties: Kent Belle (24 in./60 cm, purple-violet), Sarastro (24 in./60 cm, very large, dark violet flowers, grows runners)

Height:
*24–31 inches/
60–80 cm*
**Blooming
Time:**
June–July

Campanula persicifolia

Peach-leaved Bellflower ✿
Also Known as: Willow Bellflower

Family: Bellflower plants *(Campanulaceae)*
Native to: Europe, Caucasus, Western Siberia
Bloom: Round bellflowers in white and shades of blue on long, unbranched stalks
Appearance: Small leaves in low clusters, from which the long flower stalks grow
Location: Sun to partial shade, or bright sun, but not midday; moderately dry, loamy soils
Planting: Can be planted from spring to fall
Care: To avoid self-seeding, cut off blooms that have gone by.
Arrangement: For natural appearing flowerbeds; goes well with yellow (e.g., *Alchemilla, Aster linosyris, Buphtalmum, Euphorbia, Hemerocallis, Inula, Aster amellus,* and *Clematis recta*)
Notes: The blooms are good for cutting.
Species/Varieties: Blue Boomers (blue, semidouble), Chettle Charm (white, blue margin), Coronata Alba (white, double), Grandiflora (blue), Grandiflora Alba (white), Largo Double Blue (light blue, semidouble)

Height:
*4–6 inches/
10–15 cm*
**Blooming
Time:**
June–Aug.

Campanula portenschlagiana

Dalmatian Bellflower ❀

Family: Bellflower plants *(Campanulaceae)*
Native to: Bosnia, Croatia
Bloom: Small, abundant appearing bellflowers in shades of blue and violet; short, flowering shoots
Appearance: Fresh green carpet that slowly spreads by means of underground runners
Location: Sun to partial shade; versatile from rock garden to border of wooded area
Planting: Can be planted from spring through fall.
Care: Simply split off and dig up anything that becomes troublesome.
Arrangement: Attractive with small *Alchemilla, Ceratostigma, Dianthus, Euphorbia, Iberis, Geranium,* and *Gypsophila*
Species/Varieties: Birch Hybrid (dark purple, → illus.), Resholdt's Variety (violet); similar: *C. poscharskyana* (4–10 in./10–25 cm, good for edging), Blauranke (light blue, fast growing), E. H. Frost (white, wintergreen), Lilacina (purple-pink), Stella (violet, dark stems, wintergreen); Carpathian Bellflower, *C. carpatica* (8 in./20 cm, blue and white, June–July)

Height:
*32 inches/
80 cm*
**Blooming
Time:**
June–Aug.

Centaurea dealbata

Persian Cornflower
Also Known as: Rosea, Centurea, Perennial Cornflower

Family: Compositae *(Asteraceae)*
Native to: Caucasus
Bloom: Large, vigorous, red and pink cornflowers
Appearance: Fairly broad yet upright stature; large, lobed leaves with white hairy underside
Location: Sunny and warm; porous and fairly dry soils
Planting: Best planted in the spring
Care: Cut off blooms that have gone by for new flowers
Arrangement: Intense, impressive color that goes well with blue-gray plants such as *Echinops, Eryngium, Nepeta,* and *Scabiosa;* also attractive with *Achillea, Malva, Stachys,* and *Tanacetum*
Notes: Flowers are good for cutting.
Species/Varieties: Steenbergii (purple-red, white center, → illus.); similar: *C. bella* (12 in./30 cm, pink, June–July, gray-green foliage); *C. hypoleuca* John Coutts (24 in./60 cm, pink, June–Oct.); Yellow Hardhead or Bighead Knapweed, *C. macrocephala* (47 in./120 cm, yellow flower clusters, June–Sept.)

Height:
*16–32 inches/
40–80 cm*
**Blooming
Time:**
May–July

Centaurea montana

Mountain Bluet ✿
Also Known as: Perennial Cornflower

Family: Compositae *(Asteraceae)*
Native to: Europe
Bloom: Large cornflower-like flower heads in blue, purple, and white
Appearance: Loose, erect growth; lanceolate, hairy leaves; spreads by means of creeping rootstock
Location: Undemanding; sunny, fairly dry; light shade
Planting: Can be planted from spring to fall
Care: Cutting back after the first flowering encourages a second blooming. Don't fertilize too heavily.
Arrangement: Leaves empty spaces after flowering; good partners are thus *Achillea, Alchemilla, Aster, Coreopsis, Kalimeris, Lysimachia, Salvia, Stachys,* and *Thalictrum*
Notes: Flowers are good for cutting; quite susceptible to mildew.
Species/Varieties: Alba (16–32 in./40–80 cm, white, → illus.), Carnea (purple), Grandiflora (16–32 in./40–80 cm, blue), Rosea (32 in./80 cm, pink); similar, but annual and showier: Cornflower, *C. cyanus* Blauer Junge (35 in./90 cm, blue)

Height:
*24–28 inches/
60–70 cm*
**Blooming
Time:**
June–Sept.

Centranthus ruber

Red Valerian ✿
Also Known as: Jupiter's Beard, Fox's Brush, Keys-of-Heaven

Family: Valerian plants *(Valerianaceae)*
Native to: Europe, Northwest Africa, Syria, Turkey
Bloom: Small flowers in round umbels, white or red; very long flowering time
Appearance: Loose, bushy growth; shoots tend to be lax; narrow, lanceolate, blue-green leaves
Location: Preferably sunny and moderately dry; however, also thrives in very dry soils poor in nutrients
Planting: Seeds itself
Care: Cutting back close to the ground after the first flowering encourages a second blooming. Cut back significantly in the fall to strengthen its vitality.
Arrangement: Attractive with *Achillea, Anaphalis, Artemisia, Aster, Erigeron, Gypsophila, Iris barbata, Nepeta, Oenothera, Salvia, Sidalcea,* wild tulips, and grasses
Species/Varieties: Coccineus (raspberry red, → illus.), Rosenrot (light red), Albiflorus (white)

Height:
*10 inches/
25 cm*
**Blooming
Time:**
Aug.–Oct.

Ceratostigma plumbaginoides

Hardy Plumbago
Also Known as: Leadwort, Dwarf Plumbago

Family: Leadwort or Plumbago plants *(Plumbaginaceae)*
Native to: Western China
Bloom: Gleaming blue flowers at the end of shoots
Appearance: Ground cover, erect bushes; smooth, oval leaves that usually turn red in the fall; sprouts fairly late, grows slowly, and then spreads by means of runners
Location: Sun, possibly partial shade; the soil should be dry and porous and contain humus, sand, and lime; doesn't like damp, heavy locations
Planting: Prefers spring planting
Care: As a plant with shallow roots, Plumbago doesn't like it when the soil is worked with a hoe.
Arrangement: Since the plant is slow to sprout, combine it with spring bulbs; attractive ones are *Bergenia, Euphorbia, Nepeta, Solidago, Stachys byzantina,* and *Teucrium*
Notes: Since this plant is not winter-hardy everywhere, it should be protected with gravel, especially in cold areas.

Height:
*28 inches/
70 cm*
**Blooming
Time:**
*July–Sept./
Oct.*

Chelone obliqa

Turtlehead
Also Known as: Rose Turtlehead

Family: Figwort plants *(Scrophulariaceae)*
Native to: USA
Bloom: Unusual, individual pink or white flowers that form a broad head; very long flowering time
Appearance: Erect stems with dark green, broad, lanceolate, serrate leaves; long lived
Location: Sun; moist to damp soils rich in nutrients; likes to be in the vicinity of water; also tolerates some partial shade, brief drought, and hard soils
Planting: Can be planted from spring to fall
Care: Water during drought; cut back in fall
Arrangement: Valuable late bloomer with staying power; good companions are *Aconitum, Anemone hupehensis, Leucanthemella serotina, Monarda, Physostegia,* and *Tradescantia* plants
Notes: The blooms are good for cutting.
Species/Varieties: Alba (white); White Turtlehead, *C. glabra* (20 in./50 cm, whitish pink, May–June)

Height:
*20–39 inches/
50–100 cm*
**Blooming
Time:**
Aug.–Nov.

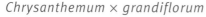

Chrysanthemum × grandiflorum

Garden Chrysanthemum
Also Known as: Garden Mum

Family: Compositae *(Asteraceae)*
Bloom: Single, semidouble, and fully double composite flowers in white, various shades of yellow, pink, red, orange, and bronze
Appearance: Erect clusters, not always entirely sturdy; deeply incised, gray-green leaves
Location: Sun; porous soil, rich in nutrients, and preferably dry; it's essential that the location not be too wet in the winter
Planting: Best planted in the spring
Care: Cover in snow-free winter; support if necessary
Arrangement: Valuable late bloomer with a large color palette; combine with such plants as *Aster, Delphinium,* and *Helenium*
Notes: The plants emit a pungent fragrance.
Species/Varieties: White Bouquet (→ illus.), Bronzekuppel (red-orange), Fellbacher Wein (wine red, semidouble), Orchid Helen (20 in./50 cm, purple-pink, double); Arctic Daisy, *Arctanthemum arcticum* (16 in./40 cm, Sept.–Oct., single flowers), Roseum (pink), Schwefelglanz (yellow)

Height:
*59–79 inches/
150–200 cm*
**Blooming
Time:** *Sept.*

Cimicifuga ramosa

Hillside Black Beauty ❈

Family: Buttercup or Crowfoot plants *(Ranunculaceae)*
Native to: Kamchatka
Bloom: Large, cream-white flower panicles
Appearance: Erect clusters with strong stems; very large, summer-green leaves, sometimes with dark coloration
Location: For half-shady, cool spots with moist to damp soils and good drainage
Planting: Long-lived, but needs a couple of years to get started
Care: Water during fairly long drought
Arrangement: The candle shape goes well with bowl-shaped flowers or panicles (e.g., *Aconitum, Anemone hupehensis)* or with ferns.
Notes: The flowers of some varieties have a delicate fragrance.
Species/Varieties: The varieties Brunette, Rotlaubig (= Atropurpurea), and Schwarzer Peter have dark leaves; Bugbane, *C. dahurica* (71 in./180 cm, July–Aug., slightly hanging); October Silberkerze, *C. simples* (51–55 in./130–140 cm, Oct., slightly pendent), White Pearl

Height:
*20–39 inches/
50–100 cm*
**Blooming
Time:**
July–Aug.

Clematis integrifolia

Solitary Clematis

Family: Buttercup or Crowfoot plants *(Ranunculaceae)*
Native to: Europe, Northern Africa, Central Asia
Bloom: Nodding flowers in purple-blue with a white center, from which downy multiple fruits develop in the fall
Appearance: Develops long shoots, but doesn't climb
Location: Full sun to sheltered from direct sun during the hottest part of the day; normal garden soil
Planting: The best time to plant is August and September.
Care: Provide support for low varieties, or lean them against other plants to guide them upward.
Arrangement: Good for border, but also in flowerbed, for example, with *Aster, Astrantia, Crambe, Echinops,* and *Eryngium*
Notes: The flowers have a delicate fragrance.
Species/Varieties: Many varieties, such as, Ernest Markham (red); Clematis, *C. × jouiniana* (July–Sept.), Mrs. Robert Brydon (20–47 in./50–120 cm, blue-white, hanging shoots); *C. heracleifolia* (July–Sept., in different varieties); Ground Clematis, *C. recta* (June–July), Purpurea (51 in./130 cm, white, purple frosted leaves)

Height:
*16–35 inches/
4–90 cm*
**Blooming
Time:**
June–Sept.

Coreopsis grandiflora

Bigflower Coreopsis
Also Known as: Large-flowered Tickseed

Family: Compositae *(Asteraceae)*
Native to: USA, Northern Mexico
Bloom: Large, yellow composite flowers that appear tireless
Appearance: Bushy growth; the flower stems rise above the foliage; narrow, lanceolate, summer-green leaves
Location: Sun; moist, porous soils rich in nutrients
Planting: Prefers planting in the spring
Care: Relatively short-lived perennial; prolong by cutting it back significantly in the fall to encourage formation of buds
Arrangement: Goes well with blue flowers such as *Aster, Delphinium, Eryngium, Pseudolysimachion longifolium,* and *Salvia*
Notes: The blooms last a long time in the vase.
Species/Varieties: Cutting Gold (28–35 in./70–90 cm, golden yellow, → illus.), Domino (16 in./40 cm, yellow, black center), Early Sunrise (16 in./40 cm, semidouble); similar: *C. lanceolate:* Baby Sun (16 in./40 cm, golden yellow), Little Red Hen (6 in./15 cm, yellow, brown eye)

Height:
*12–24 inches/
30–60 cm*
**Blooming
Time:**
July–Sept.

Coreopsis verticillata

Whorled Coreopsis ✿
**Also Known as: Moonbeam, Thread-leaved Tickseed,
Pot-of-Gold**

Family: Compositae *(Asteraceae)*
Native to: USA
Bloom: Yellow composite long blooms in mostly sturdy stalks
Appearance: Primarily erect shoots; fine, summer-green
needle-like foliage; the plant develops runners, but they are
not troublesome
Location: Sun; preferably in moist soils rich in nutrients; also
tolerates brief drought
Planting: Seeds itself in appropriate locations
Care: Easy to care for; cut back in the spring
Arrangement: Looks good even after blooming so it can be
placed quite far to the front of the flowerbed; attractive companions are *Aster laevis, Erigeron, Oenothera, Nepeta, Phlox
maculata, Pseudolysimachion, Rudbeckia,* and *Stachys macrantha*
Species/Varieties: Zagreb (12 in./30 cm, golden yellow, →
illus.), Grandiflora (20–24 in./50–60 cm, yellow), Moonbeam
(16 in./40 cm, light lemon-yellow, low)

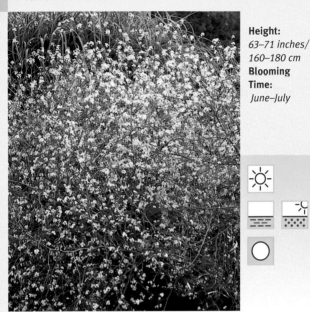

Height:
*63–71 inches/
160–180 cm*
**Blooming
Time:**
June–July

Crambe cordifolia

Colewort
Also Known as: Flowering Kale

Family: Mustard or Cabbage plants *(Brassicaceae)*
Native to: Caucasus
Bloom: Small, white blooms in imposing, loose, abundantly branched panicles reaching far over the leaves
Appearance: Very large, cabbage-like, rough, summer-green leaves; ornamental effect
Location: Sun; in loamy, moderately dry, and porous soils; also tolerates partial shade
Planting: Can be planted from spring to fall; needs lots of room
Care: Cover with soil if plants work their way out of the ground
Arrangement: Typical perennial for solitary planting; blooming time is short so it's better in the background; good companions include *Achillea, Asphodeline, Centranthus, Gypsophila, Nepeta, Phlomis, Sedum, Verbascum, Yuccan,* and grasses
Species/Varieties: Similar to Sea Kale, *C. maritima* (24 in./60 cm, white flower, gray-blue leaves)

Height:
*39–79 inches/
100–200 cm*
**Blooming
Time:**
*June–July,
Sept.*

Delphinium Elatum-group

Blue Delphinium
Also Known as: Candle Larkspur

Family: Buttercup of Crowfoot plants *(Ranunculaceae)*
Bloom: Spurred individual flowers clustered on dense, abundant spikes in a wide variety of shades of blue
Appearance: Mostly sturdy flower stalks; partly palm-sized, incised, summer-green leaves
Location: Sun; in open, well-prepared soils that are light, deep, and rich in nutrients
Planting: Can be planted from spring to fall
Care: Divide every couple of years to maintain willingness to flower; susceptible to mildew if fertilized excessively; cut back after the first flowering for second blooming.
Arrangement: A specimen plant; leaves empty space after blooming
Notes: At great risk from snails and slugs
Species/Varieties: Berghimmel (sky blue, white eye), Finster-aarhorn (deep blue, black eye), Jubelruf (medium blue, white eye); Belladonna group (28–47 in./70–120 cm, loose flower panicles); Pacific group (28–71 in. /70–180 cm)

Height:
*6–12 inches/
15–30 cm*
**Blooming
Time:**
May–July

Dianthus plumarius

Cottage Pink
Also Known as: Feathered Pink, Grass Pink, Scotch Pink

Family: Pink or Carnation plants *(Caryophyllaceae)*
Native to: Austria, Slovenia, Croatia
Bloom: Quite large, double blooms in white, pink, and red
Appearance: Mat-like growth; narrow, lanceolate, gray-green foliage; wintergreen
Location: Sun; porous, fairly dry soils containing lime
Planting: Can be planted from spring to fall
Care: Protect from dampness in the winter; fertilize only lightly
Arrangement: The low varieties are particularly good for borders. Attractive partners are *Campanula, Iberis, Geranium, Lavandula, Origanum, Sedum,* and *Thymus*
Notes: The flowers emit the typical pungent carnation scent.
Species/Varieties: Heidi (carmine), Ine (white with red), Rose du mai (pink); Fire Witch, *D. gratianopolitanus* (2–6 in./5–15 cm, compact carpet, small mostly single flowers), Eydangeri (pink), Pink Jewel (pink, semidouble); Clusterhead Pink; *D. carthusianorum* (16 in./40 cm, red, gravelly soils)

Height:
*28–32 inches/
70–80 cm*
**Blooming
Time:**
April–July

Dicentra spectabilis

Bleeding Heart

Family: Fumitory plants *(Fumariaceae)*
Native to: China, Manchuria, Korea
Bloom: Heart-shaped flower in pink with white "tear";
arranged in rows of several flowers on a hanging panicle
Appearance: Loose growth; blue-green, divided leaves from
which the flower stalks grow; comes into bloom in the summer
Location: Preferably partial shade and protected; however, it
also tolerates a little sun; moist to damp soils rich in nutrients
Planting: Plant in a protected area: plant is sensitive to frost.
Care: Cut off leaves if they turn brown.
Arrangement: Plant individually or in small groups, for they
soon leave empty spots; attractive neighbors are *Brunnera,
Campanula, Doronicum, Hemerocallis, Iris sibirica,* and *Trollius*
Species/Varieties: Alba (white); *D. eximia* (12 in./30 cm, pink
or white, May–Aug., showy, gray-green leaves, turn yellow in
the fall); *D. formosa* ssp. *formosa* (12 in./30 cm, pink, red, or
white, May–July, fern-like, gray leaves), Luxuriant (dark pink,
blue-green leaves), Stuart Boothman (dark red)

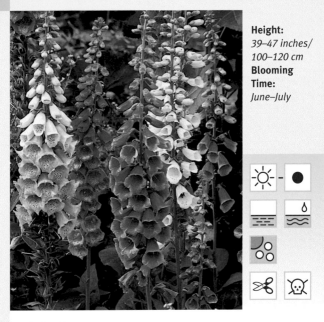

Height:
*39–47 inches/
100–120 cm*
**Blooming
Time:**
June–July

Digitalis purpurea

Purple Foxglove ✿

Family: Figwort plants *(Scrophulariaceae)*
Native to: Europe, Morocco, Madeira
Bloom: Pink, red, white nodding bells in long panicles
Appearance: Rough leaf rosettes from which individual stems grow; a short-lived perennial, but it produces lots of seeds
Location: Prefers partial to light shade; loose, moist soils containing humus; does not tolerate standing water
Planting: Usually seeds itself to different locations
Care: Cutting back after blooming strengthens vitality
Arrangement: Apt to run wild; good matches include *Aruncus, Brunnera, Campanula, Geranium, Hosta,* and ferns
Notes: The entire plant is poisonous.
Species/Varieties: Foxy (24 in./60 cm, mixture), Sutton's Apricot (salmon colored), Primrose Carousel (lemon yellow, dark spots); Rusty Foxglove, *D. ferruginea* (39–71 in./ 100–180 cm, yellow, June–Aug., short-lived, self-seeding); Large-flowered Foxglove, *D. grandiflora* (32 in./80 cm, yellow-brown, long-lived); Straw Foxglove, *D. lutea* (24–39 in./60–100 cm)

Height:
*10–20 inches/
25–50 cm*
**Blooming
Time:**
April–May

Doronicum orientale

Caucasian Leopardbane

Family: Compositae *(Asteraceae)*
Native to: Alps, Balkans, Caucasus, Lebanon, Turkey
Bloom: Yellow daisy blooms that appear early in the year
Appearance: Bushy, erect; fairly long, heart-shaped leaves
Location: Sun to partial shade; porous, moist soils containing humus
Planting: Can be planted from the spring to the fall
Care: Continually cut off blooms that have gone by to encourage new flowering; cut back after flowering
Arrangement: Still somewhat attractive after blooming, so appropriate for the middle or the rear of the flowerbed; good neighbors are *Brunnera, Dicentra, Polemonium, Primula*, bulb flowers, and later blooming species that they cover up in the summer
Notes: The blooms are good for cutting.
Species/Varieties: Finesse (20 in./50 cm), Goldzwerg (10 in./25 cm), Little Leo (14 in./35 cm, yellow, double flower wreath), Magnificum (16 in./40 cm); *D. plantagineum* (28 in./70 cm, May–June, fairly large blooms)

Height:
*24–39 inches/
60–100 cm*
**Blooming
Time:**
July–Sept.

Echinacea purpurea

Purple Coneflower
Also Known as: Hedgehog Coneflower

Family: Compositae *(Asteraceae)*
Native to: USA
Bloom: Large stand of red or white, often hanging, radiating flowers around a dome-shaped center
Appearance: Solid, nearly rigid appearing stalks; large, rough, egg-shaped leaves; fairly short-lived perennial
Location: Sun; moist soils rich in nutrients
Planting: Prefers planting in the spring
Care: Regularly cut off blooms that have gone by.
Arrangement: Goes well with lavender and smaller flowers in dark red (e.g., *Aster, Bistorta, Phlox maculata, Salvia, and Sedum*), and Bush grass, Feather Grass, and switch grass
Notes: Cut fresh blooms for the vase.
Species/Varieties: Alba (24–32 in./60–80 cm, green-white), Doppeldecker (39 in./100 cm, purple-red), Green Edge (39 in./100 cm, white-green), Magnus (32–35 in./80–90 cm, purple); *Echinacea* hybrids: Sunset (24–35 in./60–90 cm, orange), Sunrise (24–35 in./60–90 cm, yellow)

Height:
*32–63 inches/
80–160 cm*
**Blooming
Time:**
July–Sept.

Echinops ritro ssp. *ritro*

Globe Thistle

Family: Compositae *(Asteraceae)*
Native to: Europe, Caucasus, Central Asia
Bloom: Spherical flowers in blue; attractive until winter
Appearance: Long, stiff, erect flower stems; large, feathery, gray-blue leaves
Location: Sunny and warm to even hot; dry to moist, porous soils rich in nutrients
Planting: Can be planted from spring to fall
Care: Support if necessary; If you don't want the plants to seed themselves, you have to cut off the blooms that have gone by before they form seeds.
Arrangement: Plant large varieties by themselves; appropriate neighbors are *Achillea, Echinacea, Lythrum, Rudbeckia, Salvia, Veronicastrum,* and grasses such as *Miscanthus* and *Molinia*
Notes: For the vase or for drying, cut before blooming
Species/Varieties: Blue Ball (blue), Taplow Blue (intense blue), Veitch's Blue (steel blue); similar: *E. sphaerocephalus* (59 in./150 cm, gray-blue flowers, June–Aug.), Arctic Glow (32 in./80 cm, white balls, red stems, shimmering silver leaves)

Height:
*12–14 inches/
30–35 cm*
**Blooming
Time:**
April–May

Epimedium × versicolor 'Sulphureum'

Bishop's Hat ✿
Also Known as: Barrenwort

Family: Barberry plants *(Berberidaceae)*
Bloom: Large, spurred, yellow flowers in showy panicles
Appearance: Bushy, branched growth; heart-shaped leaves that turn brownish red in the fall
Location: Half-shade to shade; moist, loose soils
Planting: Can be planted from spring to fall
Care: Undemanding and long-lived in the proper locations; cut off old leaves in the spring before blooming
Arrangement: Attractive ground cover under and at the edge of woods, for example, with *Bergenia, Brunnera, Dicentra, Euphorbia,* small *Hosta, Tiarella,* and ferns
Species/Varieties: *E. grandiflorum* (8 in./20 cm, white); Lilafee (10 in./25 cm, purple), Rose Queen (12 in./30 cm, pink); *E. × perralchicum* Yellow Epimedium (12 in./30 cm, wintergreen); *E. pinnatum* Elegans (10 in./25 cm, yellow, wintergreen); *E. × warleyense* (8 in./20 cm, copper colors, wintergreen); *E. × youngianum* (8 in./20 cm), Lilacinum (pink-purple), Niveum (white)

Height:
*24 inches/
60 cm*
**Blooming
Time:**
*June–July,
Sept.*

Erigeron Hybrids

Fleabane ✿
Also Known as: Starwort

Family: Compositae *(Asteraceae)*
Bloom: Fine radiate blooms in blue, violet, pink, and white with yellow center; in loose bunches with multiple shoots
Appearance: The mostly sturdy flower stems stand above the leaves; lanceolate leaves in thick bunches
Location: Sun; moist to damp, porous soils rich in nutrients; does not like dampness in winter
Planting: Can be planted from spring to fall
Care: Cutting back after the first blooming encourages a second flowering in the fall.
Arrangement: Despite its early blooming, this species can be placed at the front of the flowerbed, since it flowers twice. Attractive companions are *Achillea, Coreopsis, Leucanthemum, Phlox,* and *Salvia.*
Notes: Cut for the vase when flowers are in full bloom.
Species/Varieties: Sommerneuschnee (whitish pink, → illus.), Darkest of All (violet-blue), Foerster's Liebling (carmine-pink, semidouble), Rotes Meer (dark red)

Height:
*16–32 inches/
40–80 cm*
**Blooming
Time:**
July–Aug.

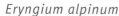

Eryngium alpinum

Alpine Sea Holly

Family: Umbellifer plants *(Apiaceae)*
Native to: France, Switzerland, Austria, Slovenia
Bloom: Blue, spadix-shaped flowers similar to thistles
Appearance: Erect; large, lobate, blue-gray leaves; very long-lived in the right location
Location: Sun; rich in nutrients; tolerates dryness; likes fairly moist soil in the spring, but no dampness in the winter
Planting: Doesn't like to be crowded
Care: As long as the location is right, the plant is long-lived.
Arrangement: *Achillea, Aster,* and *Solidago* are good companions.
Notes: Good for the vase and for drying
Species/Varieties: Amethyst (silver-blue, → illus.), Blue Star (deep blue), Opal (silver-violet); Pyrenees Sea Holly, *E. bourgatii* (16 in./40 cm, steel blue, July–Aug., leaves have white veins); Miss Wilmot's Ghost, *E. giganteum:* (28–35 in./70–90 cm, silver-green, biennial, seeds itself); Flat Sea Holly, *E. planum* 20–28 in./50–70 cm, deep blue, June–Aug.)

Height:
*59–98 inches/
150–250 cm*
**Blooming
Time:**
Aug.–Sept.

Eupatorium maculatum

Joe-pye Weed ✿
Also Known as: Boneset

Family: Compositae *(Asteraceae)*
Native to: Canada, USA
Bloom: Small, pink or white flowers in sumptuous umbels
Appearance: Erect, clustered growth; lanceolate, slightly toothed leaves; imposing structure
Location: Sun to partial shade; moist to damp, porous soil; likes to be near water
Planting: Can be planted from spring to fall
Care: Support if necessary; water during fairly long drought
Arrangement: Use individual plants with such companions as *Bistorta, Chelone, Lysimachia, Lythrum, Vernonia,* and *Veronicastrum* and grasses such as *Miscanthus*
Species/Varieties: Atropupureum (dark red, → illus.); Hollow-stemmed Joe-pye Weed, *E. fistulosum* (71 in./180 cm), Atropupureum (wine red); Hemp Agrimony, *E. cannabinum* (59 in./150 cm), Plenum (pink, double); Sweet Joe-pye Weed, *E. purpureum* (71 in./180 cm); White Snake Root, *Ageratina altissima* Chocolate (32–39 in./80–100 cm, white, red-brown leaf)

Height:
16–20 inches/
40–50 cm
**Blooming
Time:**
April–May

Euphorbia amygdaloides

Wood Spurge

Family: Spurge plants *(Euphorbiacea)*
Native to: Europe, Caucasus, Northern Iran, Northern Africa
Bloom: Small flowers in large umbels; the yellow-green upper leaves are more impressive than the flowers
Appearance: Loose, bushy growth; lanceolate, wintergreen, reddish leaves; reddish stems; attractive nearly year-round
Location: Half to full shade; likes soils containing lime
Planting: Can be planted from spring to fall
Care: Cover during the winter in cold locations
Arrangement: Good neighbors include other spring bloomers such as *Brunnera, Cyclamen, Epimedium, Helleborus, Hosta,* and *Tiarella.* Light-colored flowers go well with the dark leaves.
Notes: The white, milky sap is irritating to skin.
Species/Varieties: Purpurea (red-leafed, → illus.), Aurea (yellow-leafed); *E. robbiae* (16 in./40 cm, wintergreen); *E. polychroma* (16 in./40 cm, yellow, June–Aug.); Cypress Spurge, *E. cyparissias* (6 in./15 cm, yellow-green, May–June, needle-shaped leaves)

Height:
*24–32 inches/
60–80 cm*
**Blooming
Time:**
April–July

Euphorbia characias ssp. *wulfenii*

Mediterranean Spurge

Family: Spurge plants *(Euphorbiaceae)*
Native to: Southwestern Europe, Northern Africa
Bloom: Very large, thick flower umbels consisting of individual small, yellow flowers
Appearance: Massive, with leaves all around the stems, which are not always erect; gray-green leaves; wintergreen
Location: Sunny, warm, and protected; preferably in dry, porous soils poor in nutrients
Planting: Can be planted from spring to fall
Care: Protect from frost in cold locations; support shoots
Arrangement: Specimen plant that remains attractive even after flowering; looks good with *Artemisia, Centaurea, Geranium,* tall *Nepeta,* and *Salvia;* if possible, support with appropriate neighboring plants
Notes: In sunlight, the milky sap is a skin irritant.
Species/Varieties: *E. characias* ssp. *characias,* Blue Wonder (24 in./60 cm, blue-green leaves, compact), Forescate (16 in./40 cm, low)

Height:
31–39 inches/ 80–100 cm
Blooming Time:
May–June

Euphorbia griffithii
Fireglow

Family: Spurge plants *(Euphorbiaceae)*
Bloom: Orange-red apetalous flowers on erect shoots that turn reddish in the fall
Appearance: Sturdy, erect growth; lanceolate leaves, all orange-red; forms light runners
Location: Sun to partial shade and protected; prefers damp, loose soils rich in nutrients
Planting: Can be planted from spring to fall
Care: In the first year, cover over in winter
Arrangement: Impressive areas of color; blue and violet intensify; attractive with *Alchemilla, Bergenia, Helleborus,* and *Tiarella*
Notes: In sunlight, the milky sap is a skin irritant.
Species/Varieties: Fireglow (orange-red, → illus.), Dixter (= Great Dixter, intense orange-red); for damp, sunny to half-shady locations: Marsh Spurge, *E. palustris* (39 in./100 cm, yellow-green, May–June, stand of flowers looks attractive through fall, reddish fall coloring, easy to care for); varieties are rarely available commercially

Height:
*39–59 inches/
100–150 cm*
**Blooming
Time:**
July–Aug.

Filipendula rubra

Queen of the Prairie

Family: Roses *(Rosaceae)*
Native to: USA
Bloom: Loose umbels with small, individual pink flowers
Appearance: Erect flower stems; large, hand-shaped, summer-green leaves; still appealing even after flowering
Location: Sun; moist to damp ground rich in nutrients; also tolerates partial shade and brief drought
Planting: Can be planted from spring to fall
Care: Water during prolonged periods of drought; continually cut off blooms that have gone by.
Arrangement: Specimen plant due to its tremendous size; attractive with *Bistorta, Leucanthemella, Lysimachia clethroides, Rudbeckia laciniata, Veronica,* and *Veronicastrum*
Species/Varieties: Venusta (59 in./150 cm, → illus.), Venusta Magnifica (59 in./150 cm, dark pink); *F. palmata* (32 in./80 cm, pink, June–July, fragrant, feathery leaves); *F. purpurea*: (July–Aug.); varieties: Alba (24 in./60 cm, white), Elegans (28 in./70 cm, carmine); *F. vulgaris* Plena (12 in./30 cm, creamy white, double, fern-like leaves)

Height:
*10–20 inches/
25–50 cm*
**Blooming
Time:**
July–Sept.

Gaillardia aristata

Common Gaillarda
Also Known as: Blanket Flower

Family: Compositae *(Asteraceae)*
Native to: Northern and Southwestern USA
Bloom: Large composite in shades of yellow and red, usually bicolor with a red center
Appearance: Bushy, erect growth with abundant clusters of leaves; fairly short-lived
Location: Sun; preferably in dry, porous soils rich in nutrients; usually lives longer on sandy soils
Planting: Prefers spring planting
Care: Cutting back significantly in the fall encourages formation of buds for wintering over and increases lifespan
Arrangement: Best planted with yellow and brownish red (e.g., *Aster linosyris, Achillea, Calendula,* and *Coreopsis*)
Species/Varieties: Arizona Sun (12–16 in./30–40 cm, yellow with red center), Burgunder (28 in./70 cm, brown-red), Fackelschein (28 in./70 cm, red, yellow rim), Kobold (10 in./25 cm, red-yellow), Tokajer (28 in./70 cm, orange)

Height:
8–12 inches/
20–30 cm
Blooming Time:
May–July

Geranium × cantabrigiense

St. Ola ✿

Family: Cranesbill plants *(Geraniaceae)*
Bloom: Small, white or pink bowl-like flowers consisting of five flower petals that appear numerous
Appearance: Low, bushy growth that becomes expansive over time; smooth, wintergreen, lobate, rounded leaves; turns color in the fall
Location: Sun to partial shade; fairly dry, porous soils
Planting: Can be planted from spring to fall
Care: Very easy to care for
Arrangement: In the foreground of beds or the top of walls with such plants as *Campanula, Dianthus, Iberis, Nepeta, Salvia,* and *Saponaria;* also attractive at the edge of a wooded area
Notes: The leaves have a tangy fragrance.
Species/Varieties: Berggarten (pearl pink, → illus.), Biokovo (white-pink), Cambridge (dark pink), Karmina (dark pink-purple); *G. cinereum* (8–10 in./20–25 cm, pink or red, June–Sept.); *G. dalmaticum* (4–6 in./10–15 cm, white or pink, June–Sept.); *G. renardii* (8–10 in./20–30 cm, white or pink, June–July)

Height:
*12–20 inches/
30–50 cm*
**Blooming
Time:**
June–Sept.

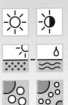

Geranium endressii

Wargrave's Pink ✿

Family: Cranesbill plants *(Geraniaceae)*
Native to: Spain, France
Bloom: Slightly funnel-shaped flowers in shades of pink
Appearance: Bushy growth, tends to collapse; fresh green, deeply incised leaves with rough upper surface
Location: Sun to partial shade; loose, moist to damp or even dry soils rich in nutrients
Planting: Can be planted from spring to fall
Care: Cut back after the first flowering for a second blooming
Arrangement: Good at the edge of wooded areas with *Aster laevis, Campanula, Digitalis,* and other *Geranium* species
Species/Varieties: The varieties are often classified as *G. oxonianum*: Claridge Bruce (pink-purple), Rosenlicht (pink-red), Wageningen (pink, low plant), Wargrave Pink (dark pink); *G. versicolor* (16–24 in./40–60 cm, light pink, veined flowers, June–Aug., also in white); *G. phaeum* (16–35 in./40–90 cm, May–July, tolerates dryness); David Bromley (white-gray with violet)

Height:
*12–24 inches/
30–60 cm*
**Blooming
Time:**
May–July

Geranium himalayense

Himalayan Geranium ✿

Family: Cranesbill plants *(Geraniaceae)*
Native to: Afghanistan, Kashmir, Northwest India, Nepal
Bloom: Single or double bowl-shaped flowers in various shades of blue and purple
Appearance: Clustered growth; spreads by means of runners; leaves deeply divided; in the fall they turn yellow to light orange (depending on location)
Location: Partial shade and fairly cool; porous and moist to moderately dry soils
Planting: Can be planted from spring to fall
Care: Cut back significantly after flowering
Arrangement: On cool borders or at the edge of wooded areas, with such plants as *Alchemilla, Astilbe, Campanula,* and *Paeonia*
Species/Varieties: Grevetye (blue with purple veins, → illus.), Baby Blue (blue-purple, low plant), Birch Double (violet, double), Johnsonn's Blue (blue-purple); *G. × magnificum* (16–24 in./40–60 cm, dark violet, May–June, hairy leaves, turn red-orange in the fall, tolerates dry locations)

Height:
*8–14 inches/
20–35 cm*
**Blooming
Time:**
May–July

Geranium macrorrhizum

Bigroot Geranium ✿

Family: Cranesbill plants *(Geraniaceae)*
Native to: Southern and Eastern Europe
Bloom: White, light to dark pink, or red bowl-shaped flower
Appearance: Bushy growth; spreads extensively through rhizomes; slightly divided, hairy leaves; the older leaves in particular turn reddish in the fall; in the spring the new leaves grow over the older ones
Location: Preferably partial shade and moist ground, but can also tolerate sun, shade, and dry conditions
Planting: Can be planted from spring through fall
Care: Extremely easy to care for
Arrangement: Spreading under wooded areas or in small clusters with *Aruncus, Epimedium, Tellima,* and *Geranium* species
Notes: The leaves emit a very special scent.
Species/Varieties: Czakor (red), Ingwersen (soft pink, but usually sold with dark pink flowers), Mytikas (dark pink), Spessart (white with a touch of pink), Variegatum (light pink, yellow variegated leaves, slow growth)

Height:
12–47 inches/
30–120 cm
**Blooming
Time:**
July–Sept.

Geranium psilostemon

Armenian Cranesbill

Family: Cranesbill plants *(Geraniaceae)*
Native to: Northeastern Turkey, Southwestern Caucasus
Bloom: Bowl-shaped flowers with a dark eye, in intense, glowing pink or magenta
Appearance: Clumped growth; the tallest varieties tend to collapse; large, lobate leaves
Location: Sun to partial shade; moist soils rich in nutrients and containing little lime
Planting: Can be planted from spring to fall
Care: If necessary, support the clusters; cut back significantly after flowering so the plant can gather its strength for the winter; in cold areas, cover for the winter
Arrangement: Impressive color; goes well with *Campanula* and *Phlox*
Species/Varieties: Hybrids containing some *G. psilostemon:* Ann Folkard (dark magenta, June–Sept.), Patricia (magenta, July–Sept.); other hybrids: Brookside (blue, white eye, June–July), Philippe Vapelle (blue-violet, June–July), Ann Thomson (pink, June–Sept.)

Height:
*8–16 inches/
20–40 cm*
**Blooming
Time:**
June–Sept.

Geranium sanguineum

Bloody Cranesbill Geranium ✽

Family: Cranesbill plants *(Geraniaceae)*
Native to: Europe, Caucasus, Turkey
Bloom: Single bowl-shaped flower in red, pink, purple, or white
Appearance: Broad, bushy growth; fine, deeply incised leaves that turn red in the fall; long vines
Location: Sun to partial shade and warm; moderately dry to moist soils containing lime and clay; also thrives in hot locations
Planting: Can be planted from spring to fall
Care: Cut back all shoots in the spring
Arrangement: Attractive in small groups with panicles or spikes of flowers such as *Campanula persicifolia, Lysimachia clethroides, Pseudolysimachion, Salvia, Sedum,* and *Stachys*
Species/Varieties: Apfelblüte (light pink), Aviemore (pink), Cedric Morris (pale red), Elsbeth (pink-red), Glenluce (soft purple-pink), Max Frei (violet-red); *G. sanguineum* hybrids: Dilys (red-violet, July–Sept.), Diva (violet-pink), Khan (intense violet-red, June–Aug.), Tiny Monster (red)

Height:
12–24 inches/
30–60 cm
Blooming Time:
May–July

Geranium sylvaticum

Woodland Geranium ✿
Also Known as: Wood Cranesbill

Family: Cranesbill plants *(Geraniaceae)*
Native to: Europe to Western Asia
Bloom: Bowl-shaped flower in shades of blue or red violet
Appearance: Clustered growth; taller varieties are prone to collapse; deeply cut, hand-shaped lobate leaves
Location: Half- to light shade and cool; moist to damp soils rich in nutrients and containing clay
Planting: Can be planted from spring to fall
Care: Support with neighboring plants; for a second flowering, cut back significantly after the first
Arrangement: For natural plantings (e.g., with *Alchemilla, Bergenia, Campanula, Euphorbia, Filipendula, Ligularia, Lysimachia, Lythrum, Stachys macrantha,* and *Trollius*)
Species/Varieties: Mayflower (blue-violet with light center; → illus.), Amy Doncaster (deep blue), Birch Lilac (blue-purple), Album (white); Purple Haze, *G. pratense* (20–24 in./50–60 cm, June–July), Albiflorum (white), Mrs. Kendall Clarke (light blue with dark veins)

Height:
*12–20 inches/
30–50 cm*
**Blooming
Time:**
June–Sept.

Geum chiloense

Geum quellyon
Also Known as: Avens

Family: Rose plants *(Roseaceae)*
Native to: Chile
Bloom: Single, semidouble blooms in yellow, orange, and red
Appearance: Forms rosettes of leaves; blooms and leaves
resemble those of strawberries; not very long-lived
Location: Half-shade; moist to damp soils rich in nutrients
Planting: Can be planted from spring to fall
Care: Remove wilted parts to lengthen blooming time.
Arrangement: Luminous colors; go well with yellow and blue
(e.g., with *Achillea, Alchemilla, Asphodeline, Aster, Brunnera,
Campanula, Doronicum, Filipendula, Geranium,* and *Nepeta*)
Species/Varieties: Feuerball (= Lady Stratheden, red, semi-
double, → illus.), Goldball (= Mrs. Bradshaw, golden yellow,
semidouble), Princess Juliane (yellow-orange, semidouble,
long-lasting); Werner Arends, *G. coccineum* (12 in./30 cm,
June–Sept.); Album (white), Leonard (copper-red)

Height:
12–39 inches/ 30–100 cm
Blooming Time:
June–Sept.

Gypsophila paniculata

Baby's Breath
Also Known as: Bristol Fairy

Family: Carnation plants *(Caryophyllaceae)*
Native to: Central and Eastern Europe, Central Asia
Bloom: Small, single or double flowers in loose, cloudy appearing panicles
Appearance: Bushy growth; small, lanceolate, summer-green leaves; often not very long-lasting
Location: Sun; porous, preferably sandy and fairly dry soils; doesn't like dampness in the winter
Planting: Can be planted from spring to fall
Care: Provide support if necessary; protect from winter dampness
Arrangement: Attractive hazy effect with larger flowers such as *Achillea, Aster, Knautia, Lavandula, Nepeta,* and *Salvia*
Notes: Flowers can be cut and kept.
Species/Varieties: Compacta Plena (white, double, → illus.), Bristol Fairy (white, double), Flamingo (whiteish pink), Schneeflocke (fairly low); Creeping Baby's Breath, *G. repens* (4 in./10 cm, white, May–Aug.), Pink Beauty (dark pink)

Height:
*28–59 inches/
70–150 cm*
**Blooming
Time:**
July–Sept.

Helenium Hybrids

Sneezeweed ✿
Also Known as: Helen's Flower, Dogtooth Daisy

Family: Compositae *(Asteraceae)*
Bloom: Broad, slightly pendent flowers on branched stems in yellow, red, or reddish brown, with brown or yellow center
Appearance: Sturdy, erect stems; small, lanceolate, slightly toothed, summer-green leaves
Location: Sun; moist soils
Planting: Avoid planting too close together
Care: If plants are slow to bloom, dig them up and divide them
Arrangement: Do not crowd; goes well with *Aster, Buphtalmum, Boltonia, Erigeron, Helianthus, Monarda,* and *Phlox*
Notes: The blooms last very well in a vase.
Species/Varieties: Zimbelstern (yellow with brown, → illus.), Die Blonde (yolk yellow, fringed), Moerheim Beauty (brown-red), Rubinzwerg (red), Waltraut (golden brown); Bigelow's Sneezeweed, *H. bigelovii* The Bishop (24 in./60 cm, yellow, black center, July–Aug.); Orange Sneezeweed, *H. hoopesii* (28 in./70 cm, orange-yellow, May–June)

Height:
*47–59 inches/
120–150 cm*
**Blooming
Time:**
Aug.–Sept.

Helianthus decapetalus

Thin-leaved Sunflower

Family: Compositae *(Asteraceae)*
Native to: Canada, USA
Bloom: Large, yellow daisy blooms on branched stems
Appearance: Erect, clumped growth; pointed, ovate summer-green leaves
Location: Sun; moist to damp, well-drained soils rich in nutrients
Planting: Can be planted from spring to fall
Care: Divide if flowering decreases or the center of the cluster becomes thin; water during drought
Arrangement: Specimen plant for the fall; goes well with tall *Aster, Boltonia, Echinops, Eupatorium, Helenium, Verbena,* and *Vernonia*
Notes: Cut new blooms for the vase
Species/Varieties: Capenoch Star (yellow, single, → illus.), Meteor (golden yellow, semidouble), Soleil d'or (golden yellow, double); *H. microcaphalus* (64 in./160 cm, yellow, Sept.–Oct.), Lemon Queen (59 in./150 cm, lemon yellow, Aug.–Sept.), Miss Mellish (59–71 in./150–180 cm, golden yellow, Sept.–Oct.)

97

Height:
*47–59 inches/
120–150 cm*
Blooming Time:
July–Sept.

Heliopsis helianthoides var. *scabra*

Summer Sun

Family: Compositae *(Asteraceae)*
Native to: Canada, USA
Bloom: Like small sunflowers, some semi- or fully double
Appearance: Bushy, upright clusters, not always sturdy; ovate to lanceolate, rough leaves
Location: Sun; porous soils rich in nutrients and not too dry
Planting: Can be planted from spring to fall.
Care: Water during significant drought; blooms longer if flowers that have gone by are continually cut off; provide support if necessary
Arrangement: Harmonious additions are yellow flowers such as *Helenium* and *Solidago*; provide attractive contrasts with dark blue and purple (e.g., *Aster, Delphinium, Vernonia*)
Notes: Blooms are good for cutting.
Species/Varieties: Golden Plume (golden yellow, double), Goldgrünherz (yellow with green center, double), Mars (golden yellow), Ballerina (orange-yellow, semidouble), Summer Nights (yellow, orange center, red stem)

Height:
*12–16 inches/
30–40 cm*
**Blooming
Time:**
Feb.–April

Helleborus orientalis

Lenten Rose ✿

Family: Buttercup or Crowfoot plants *(Ranunculaceae)*
Bloom: Multiple, nodding, white-green, pink, or red blooms on branched stems
Appearance: Large, deeply incised leaves, wintergreen, appear after blooming; grow slowly
Location: For partial shade; porous soils containing lime; not too damp (except in the spring), also tolerates temporary drought
Planting: Can be planted from spring to fall
Care: Do not transplant; do not hoe around roots
Arrangement: Goes well with *Brunnera, Cyclamen, Euphorbia, Omphalodes, Pulmonaria, Vinca,* and grasses such as *Carex*
Notes: All parts of the plant are poisonous.
Species/Varieties: Many varieties, different species: Christmas Rose, *H. niger* (12 in./30 cm, white, Dec.–Feb., more demanding); Stinking Hellebore or Bear's Foot, *H. foetidus* (20 in./50 cm, light green, Jan.–April, indigenous); *H. purpurascens* (16 in./40 cm, purple)

Height:
*24–39 inches/
60–100 cm*
**Blooming
Time:**
June–Sept.

Hemerocallis Hybrids

Daylily ✿

Family: Daylily *(Hemerocallidaceae)*
Bloom: Small to large funnel-shaped bloom in cream, yellow, pink, red, orange, often multicolored; double, with pleated, keeled flower petals; individual flowers last only a day
Appearance: Cluster of leaves resembling grass, which remains attractive even after flowering; the sturdy flower stems stand above the leaves.
Location: Undemanding; partial shade; moist to damp soils rich in nutrients
Planting: Best planted in April
Care: Water generously shortly before and during blooming
Arrangement: The foliage offers an attractive contrast to perennials with other leaf shapes (e.g., *Coreposis, Ligularia, Lysimachia clethroides, Phlox maculata,* and Purple Rain *Salvia*)
Species/Varieties: Many varieties such as Golden Chimes (39 in./100 cm, golden yellow, small flowers), Stella d'Oro (39 in./100 cm, green-yellow, small- and large-flowered); wild species: Citron Daylily, *H. citrina* (35–39 in./90–100 cm, narrow, light yellow flowers, July–Sept., fragrant)

Height:
*16–20 inches/
40–50 cm*
**Blooming
Time:**
July–Aug.

Heuchera Hybrids

Coralbells

Family: Saxifrage plants *(Saxifragaceae)*
Bloom: Small, white and pink bells in erect panicles
Appearance: Round, heart-shaped, digitate or incised winter-green leaves in a carpet; color spectrum ranging from yellow-green and orange to various shades of red to nearly black
Location: Sun to partial shade (the multicolored leaves turn green in the shade); porous soils containing humus, not too dry
Planting: Can be planted from spring to fall
Care: Cover for the winter in cold areas
Arrangement: Good perennial for decorative foliage; good companions include *Alchemilla, Aster, Campanula, Dicentra, Gereanium, Geum, Hosta,* and *Tiarella*
Species/Varieties: Many varieties such as Crème brulée (ochre to caramel shades), Green Spice (green with a touch of silver, red veins), Purple Petticoats (dark red, wavy leaves); *H. Micrantha* Palace Purple (16 in./40 cm, cream color, July–Aug., bronze-red leaves); *H. Sanguinea* (24 in./60 cm, white or pink, May–July); *H. × brizoides* Widar (20 in./50 cm, red blooms)

Height:
*10–39 inches/
25–100 cm*
**Blooming
Time:**
June–Sept.

Hosta Species

Hosta

Family: Hosta plants *(Hostaceae)*
Native to: USA, Asia
Bloom: Sometimes fragrant, white and purple bellflowers
Appearance: Bushy growth; lanceolate to rounded leaves,
partly white or yellow, also blue-green; late sprouter
Location: Prefers partial shade to shade (partial sun); moist,
porous soils rich in nutrients
Planting: Can be planted from spring to fall
Care: Protect from slugs
Arrangement: Use large varieties individually; the others in
small groups; goes well with *Anemone, Astilbe,* and *Cimicifuga*
Notes: The leaves and flowers are good for cutting
Species/Varieties: Many varieties, some of which, like Sum
and Substance (28 in./70 cm, purple blooms, very large,
golden green leaves), are fairly resistant to slugs; Blue Plantain
Lily, *H. ventricosa* (heart-shaped, slightly wavy leaves, various
varieties); *H. plantaginea* (fragrant blooms, various varieties)

Height:
*6–10 inches/
15–25 cm*
**Blooming
Time:**
March–May

Iberis sempervirens

Perennial Candytuft

Family: Mustard or Cabbage plants *(Brassicaceae)*
Native to: Southern Europe, Turkey
Bloom: Flat, white flower umbels in great profusion
Appearance: Thick, ground-covering mat; shoots turn some-what woody; small evergreen leaves
Location: Sun to partial shade; porous, moderately dry to moist soils containing sand and humus
Planting: Can be planted from spring to fall
Care: Cut back by a third after flowering to keep it compact.
Arrangement: Good for the edges because of the evergreen leaves; goes well with *Allium, Centaurea, Dianthus, Gypsophila, Nepeta, Origanum, Pulsatilla, Sedum,* and *Tulipa*
Species/Varieties: Snowflake (10 in./25 cm, → illus.), Weisser Zwerg (Little Gem, White Dwarf) (4 in./10 cm), Winter Magic (8 in./20 cm, early bloomer), Dwarf Snowflake (6 in./15 cm, compact), Climax (12 in./30 cm, suitable for bordering flowerbed), Elfenreigen (10 in./25 cm, pink after its peak blooming), Findel (10 in./25 cm, large flowers)

Height:
71–79 inches/
180–200 cm
Blooming Time:
July–Aug.

Inula magnifica

Inula Magnifica
Also Known as: Elecampane

Family: Compositae *(Asteraceae)*
Native to: Caucasus
Bloom: Large, yellow flowers with fine petals
Appearance: Erect growth; large, broad, elliptical leaves hairy on the bottom; actively seeds itself
Location: Sun; moist to damp soils rich in nutrients; thrives in warm and cool places
Planting: Can be planted from spring to fall
Care: Doesn't look very attractive after flowering
Arrangement: For borders and sunny wooded edges; goes well with *Cosmos, Crambe, Eupatorium, Lythrum,* and *Vernonia*
Notes: The blooms are good for cutting.
Species/Varieties: Swordleaf Inula, *I. ensifolia* (8 in./20 cm, yellow radiate blooms, narrow leaves, fond of lime); Compactum variety (round, compact plant); Elfwort (Scabwort, Elf Dock), *I. helenium* (59 in./150 cm, yellow, July–Oct.)

Height:
*20–43 inches/
50–120 cm*
**Blooming
Time:**
May–June

Iris Germanica-Group

German Iris
Also Known as: Rhizomatous Iris, Bearded Iris, Flag Iris

Family: Iris plants *(Iridaceae)*
Bloom: Large blooms consisting of pendent falls, arched fleur-de-lis petals, and a so-called beard; all shades and colors, often multicolored, with pleated flower petals
Appearance: Sword-shaped, gray-green leaves
Location: Sunny and warm; sandy, porous, fairly dry soils rich in nutrients
Planting: Best planted in the fall (Aug.–Nov.); cover the rhizomes with a shallow layer of dirt
Care: Regularly cut off flowers that have gone by.
Arrangement: Since the leaves become unattractive after flowering, plant between later blooming perennials or ones that look attractive all year long, such as *Dianthus, Lavandula, Nepeta,* and *Santolina.*
Species/Varieties: Countless varieties and other groups such as *Iris* Pumila group (6–16 in./15–40 cm); Butterfly iris, *Iris-/spuria* hybrids (32–39 in./80–100 cm, June–July, for normal garden soils with no standing water)

Height:
*24–39 inches/
60–100 cm*
**Blooming
Time:**
May–June

Iris sibirica

Siberian Iris ✿

Family: Iris plants *(Iridaceae)*
Native to: Central and Eastern Europe, Caucasus, Siberia
Bloom: Smaller, more delicate blooms than the German Iris; no beard; shades of blue, white, pink; seedpods remain attractive until fall
Appearance: Forms clusters; small, reed-like leaves
Location: Undemanding; preferably sunny, damp soil; however, it tolerates normal garden soil
Planting: Can be planted from spring to fall
Care: Divide clusters if the plant stops producing blooms
Arrangement: Very versatile and still attractive after flowering; goes well with *Euphorbia palustris, Filipendula, Geranium,* and *Trollius*
Notes: Cut budding flowers for the vase
Species/Varieties: Many varieties; similar: *I. sanguinea* (24–28 in./60–70 cm, violet and white, May–June); *I. laevigata* (32 in./80 cm, blue, July–Aug.); *I. ensata* (31–39 in./80–100 cm, pink, blue, violet, June–July, prefers dryness in the winter)

Height:
*24–32 inches/
60–80 cm*
**Blooming
Time:**
July–Sept.

Kalimeris incisa

Variegated Japanese Aster

Family: Compositae *(Asteraceae)*
Native to: Siberia, China, Japan, Korea
Bloom: Bouquets of white daisy flowers
Appearance: Erect stems; toothed, lanceolate, and deeply incised leaves; summer-green
Location: Sun to light shade; any normal, moderately dry to damp garden soil
Planting: Can be planted from spring to fall
Care: Cut off wilted blooms to prolong flowering
Arrangement: Goes well with all colors; attractive with *Coreopsis, Delphinium, Hemerocallis, Phlox, Rudbeckia,* and *Salvia*
Notes: Cut for the vase while blooming
Species/Varieties: Blue Star (28 in./70 cm, blue); for sunny locations and fairly dry, porous soils: Stokes' Aster, *Stokesia laevis* (12–16 in./30–40 cm, purple or white blooms, July–Sept., protect from dampness in the winter), varieties we rarely see for sale: Blue Danube (blue), Omega Skyrocket (blue), Peach Melba (peach-cream color)

Height:
*24–32 inches/
60–80 cm*
**Blooming
Time:**
Aug.–Oct.

Kirengeshoma palmata

Yellow Wax Bells

Family: Hydrangea plants *(Hydrangeaceae)*
Native to: Japan
Bloom: Small, light yellow, nodding bellflowers in loose umbels; waxy appearance
Appearance: Bushy, erect growth; rounded leaves slightly tinged with white and resembling oak leaves, summer-green
Location: Preferably cool and shady, also partial shade; porous, fairly damp soils containing humus; doesn't like lime; becomes stunted if the location is too sunny or too dry
Planting: Prefers spring planting
Care: Cover for the winter in cold locations; if the young shoots are destroyed by a late frost, the plant will sprout again
Arrangement: Looks nice with blue (e.g., *Aconitum*) or white flowers (e.g., *Anemone hupehensis, Astilbe, Cimicifuga, Epimedium, Hosta, Phlox maculata,* and *Rodgersia*)
Notes: The plant is susceptible to slugs.
Species/Varieties: Koreana group (20 in./50 cm, slender plant)

Height:
*16–32 inches/
60–80 cm*
**Blooming
Time:**
July–Sept.

Knautia macedonica

Knautia ✿

Family: Teasel plants *(Dipsacaceae)*
Native to: Balkans, Rumania
Bloom: Small, dark red flower head
Appearance: Loose, erect growth; branched stems; folded, fairly long, summer-green leaves
Location: For sunny, moist, and porous locations rich in nutrients; also tolerates temporary drought
Planting: Can be planted from spring to fall
Care: Easy to care for
Arrangement: Attractive neighbors include *Achillea, Agastache, Aster amellus, Campanula persicifolia, Echinops, Gypsophila, Inula, Nepeta, Salvia, Scabiosa,* and *Silene chalcedonica*
Species/Varieties: Mars Midget (16 in./40 cm, ruby red, compact), Melton Pastels (up to 59 in./150 cm, blue, purple, pink, red, salmon); similar: Butterfly Blue, *Scabiosa columbaria* (16–24 in./40–60 cm, light blue flowers, June–Sept., flower for cutting), assorted varieties in blue and pink

Height:
20–39 inches
50–100 cm
Blooming Time:
July–Sept.

Kniphofia Hybrids

Torch Lily
Also Known as: Red Hot Poker

Family: Asphodel plants *(Asphodelaceae)*
Bloom: Flower umbels in shades of orange, red, and yellow
Appearance: Clusters with reed-like leaves; not very long-lived
Location: Sun; moist to damp soils; keep dry in the winter
Planting: Plant in the spring
Care: In the winter, protect against frost and excessive moisture with leaf mulch, preferably before the leaves bind together; in the spring, cut back by about a third
Arrangement: The composite flowers look best with other shapes and with shades of yellow and blue, such as *Achillea filipendulina, Delphinium, Helenium,* and *Rudbeckia*
Notes: The blooms are good for cutting.
Species/Varieties: Royal Standard (39 in./100 cm, light yellow underneath, fire red on top, → illus.), Flamenco (32 in./80 cm, mixture of yellow, orange, and red, often bicolor), Alcazar (36 in./90 cm, fire red), Percy's Pride (28 in./70 cm, light yellow), Sunningdale Yellow (20 in./50 cm, golden yellow, smaller and blooms earlier)

Height:
*6–10 inches/
15–25 cm*
**Blooming
Time:**
May–June

Lamium maculatum

Spotted Dead Nettle ✿

Family: Mint plants *(Lamiaceae)*
Native to: Europe, Turkey, Caucasus, Northern Iran
Bloom: Small, pink or white lipped flowers
Appearance: Small leaves similar to nettles with more or less
pronounced white markings; forms small runners
Location: Partial shade to light shade; loose, moist to damp
soils containing humus; not too much lime
Planting: Can be planted from spring to fall
Care: Easy to care for
Arrangement: Don't use on excessively large surfaces; goes
with *Aquilegia, Astilbe, Brunnera, Corydalis, Geranium, Helle-
borus, Hosta, Pulmonaria,* ferns, and shade grasses
Species/Varieties: Chequers (purple-pink, → illus.), Beacon
Silver (= Silbergroschen, soft purple), Red Nancy (dark pink),
White Nancy (white, silver-white leaf); Dead Nettle, *L. orvaia*
(16 in./40 cm, erect shoots, large leaves and flowers in dark
pink); Golden Dead Nettle, *L. galeobdolon* (6–8 in./15–20
cm, yellow flowers, white-spotted leaf, spreading, large, fast
growing)

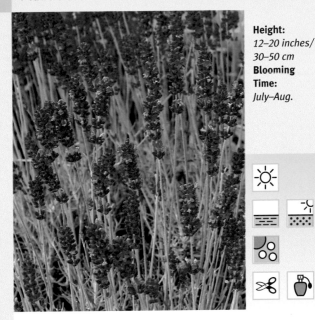

Height:
*12–20 inches/
30–50 cm*
**Blooming
Time:**
July–Aug.

Lavandula angustifolia

Lavender

Family: Mint family *(Lamiaceae)*
Native to: Southern and Western Europe
Bloom: Small, blue, violet, pink, or white flowers in thick panicles on upright stalks
Appearance: Depending on the variety, compact to loose bushes; evergreen, small, lanceolate leaves in gray-green to gray
Location: Sunny and warm; on fairly dry and preferably sandy soils containing lime
Planting: Can be planted from spring to fall
Care: Cut back significantly after flowering or in the spring (never in the fall) in order to keep the bushes compact
Arrangement: Attractive with other gray-leafed species, and with white and pink (or pink and red); appropriate for the foreground of the flowerbed
Notes: Flowers and leaves emit a strong fragrance.
Species/Varieties: Hidcote Blue (dark purple, → illus.), Grappenhall (medium blue), Hidcote Pink (pink), Munstead (medium blue)

Height:
*59 inches/
150 cm*
**Blooming
Time:**
July–Sept.

Lavatera thuringiaca

Lavatera
Also Known as: Shrub Mallow, Gay Mallow, Burgundy Wine

Family: Mallow plants *(Malvaceae)*
Native to: Central and Eastern Europe, Siberia, Central Asia
Bloom: Large, mallow-like flowers in gleaming pink
Appearance: Bushy growth; abundantly branched, erect stems; summer-green lobed leaves; relatively short-lived—to the age of three or four; fairly winter-hardy
Location: Sunny and warm; moderately dry to moist soils rich in nutrients and containing humus
Planting: Prefers spring planting
Care: Cutting back after blooming stimulates the formation of new flower shoots; cover up the base in winter
Arrangement: Suited for individual planting; goes well with *Centaurea, Delphinium, Leucanthemum, Nepeta,* and *Solidago*
Species/Varieties: *Lavatera-Olibia* hybrids (39–71 in./100–180 cm, July–Sept., need protection in winter); Barnsley varieties (white with pink, → illus.), Breddon Spring (dark pink), Burgundy Wine (wine red), Ice Cool (white), Rosea (dark pink)

Height:
20–35 inches/
50–90 cm
**Blooming
Time:**
June–Sept.

Leucanthemum × superbum

Shasta Daisy

Family: Compositae *(Asteraceae)*
Bloom: White daisy flower, single, semi- to fully double
Appearance: Erect, clustered growth; lanceolate leaves
Location: Sun; porous soils rich in nutrients
Planting: Can be planted from spring to fall
Care: Growth and flowering can be encouraged by digging plants up every three years and dividing them.
Arrangement: Goes with all colors, but particularly well with *Aster, Delphinium, Gypsophila, Lupinus, Papaver, Phlox,* and *Salvia*
Notes: Durable cut flower
Species/Varieties: Christine Hagemann (semidouble), Goldrush (light yellow, semidouble), Wirral Supreme (thick double); Oxeye Daisy, *L. vulgare* (24 in./60 cm, white, single blooming, May–June); Painted Daisy, *Tanacetum coccineum* (May–July, single blooming), E. M. Robinson (28 in./70 cm, pink), Laurin (10 in./25 cm, salmon), Regent (28 in./70 cm, glistening red), Roter Zwerg (10 in./25 cm, cherry red)

Height:
*16–35 inches/
40–90 cm*
**Blooming
Time:**
July–Aug./Sept.

Liatris spicata

Blazing Star

Family: Compositae *(Asteraceae)*
Native to: Canada, USA
Bloom: Small, violet or white flowers in candle-like heads that bloom from top to bottom
Appearance: Sturdy, upright clusters; the stems have grass-like leaves all the way to the top
Location: Sun; more or less moist soils rich in nutrients; tolerates lots of dryness, but suffers from moisture in the winter; likes sandy soils
Planting: Can be planted from spring to fall
Care: Remove blooms that have gone by
Arrangement: With contrasting flower shapes in yellow, white, and pink; attractive companions are *Anaphalis, Anthemis, Aster,* and *Coreopsis*
Notes: Good for cutting; slugs eat the leaves, voles eat the roots
Species/Varieties: Floristan Violet (28–35 in./70–90 cm, violet) and Floristan White (28–35 in./70–90 cm, white) are particularly good for cutting, Alba (24 in./60 cm, pure white), Kobold (16 in./40 cm, purple)

Height:
*71–79 inches/
180–200 cm*
**Blooming
Time:**
July–Aug.

Ligularia stenocephala

The Rocket

Family: Compositae *(Asteraceae)*
Native to: Japan, Northern China, Taiwan
Bloom: Small, yellow flowers in long spikes
Appearance: Leaf clusters up to 20 in./50 cm high; erect flower stems project upward; large, kidney-shaped leaves
Location: For light (half) shade; likes to be near water; with enough dampness in the soil, also tolerates sun
Planting: Can be planted from spring to fall
Care: Water during prolonged drought
Arrangement: Plant in small groups with other yellow or blue (violet) flowers (e.g., *Aconitum, Hemerocallis, Iris sibirica, Telekia,* and *Trollius*)
Species/Varieties: The Rocket (yellow, notched leaves, → illus.), Golden Scepter (golden yellow, rounded leaves); *L. dentata* (39–47 in./100–120 cm, Aug.–Oct., flowers in umbels), Desdemona (dark orange), Orange Queen (orange-yellow); *L. hessei* (71 in./180 cm, golden yellow, July–Aug., large, round leaves)

Height:
*16–20 inches/
40–60 cm*
**Blooming
Time:**
July–Aug.

Limonium latifolium

Sea Lavender
Also Known as: Statice Latifolia

Family: Plumbago plants *(Plumbaginaceae)*
Native to: Eastern Europe
Bloom: Small, violet flowers in hazy panicles
Appearance: Oval leaves in rosettes close to the ground, from which the broadly branched flower stalks grow
Location: Sunny and warm; preferably in fairly dry soils; also tolerates normal garden soil, however
Planting: Best not to transplant
Care: Do not water on normal soil
Arrangement: Attractive hazy effect with larger white, pink, blue, or violet flowers (e.g., *Anaphalis, Achillea, Centaurea, Erigeron, Eryngium, Iris, Sedum,* and *Stachus*)
Notes: The inflorescences are also good for drying.
Species/Varieties: Pioneer (dark violet); *L. gmelinii* (24 in./ 60 cm, lavender blue veil of flowers, July–Aug., protruding growth); related species: Tartarian Statice, *Goniolimon tataricum* (12–24 in./30–60 cm, whitish pink, July–Sept.)

Height:
*20–32 inches/
50–80 cm*
**Blooming
Time:**
July–Sept.

Linaria purpurea

Purple Toadflax

Family: Leadwort plants *(Scrophulariaceae)*
Native to: Italy, especially Sicily
Bloom: Small, pink or white flowers in narrow spikes
Appearance: Small, slender, erect clusters; gray-green, needle-shaped leaves in erect shoots; quite short-lived, but seeds itself and forms underground runners
Location: Sun, partial to light shade; feels most at home in porous, dry to moderately moist soils rich in nutrients
Planting: Seeds itself in appropriate locations
Care: Don't give additional water
Arrangement: Plant individually or in small groups; attractive near *Aster, Calamintha, Echinacea, Erigeron, Nepeta, Papaver nudicaule, Salvia,* and *Scabiosa*
Species/Varieties: Alba (white), Canon Went (pink), Springside White (white, not always available commercially); related species: Cape Fuchsia, *Phygelius capensis* (32–35 in./80–90 cm, coral-red flowers in panicles, July–Sept., sensitive to winter dampness)

Height:
*10–20 inches/
25–50 cm*
**Blooming
Time:**
June–Aug.

Linum perenne

Blue Flax

Family: Flax plants *(Linaceae)*
Native to: Europe, Turkey, Siberia
Bloom: Sky blue, loose cymes; erect stems; individual flowers last only a short time, but there are always new ones
Appearance: Loose growth; narrow, needle-shaped leaves; usually short-lived; frequently seeds itself
Location: Sunny, warm; porous, sandy soils
Planting: Can be planted from spring to fall
Care: Best left alone; protect from strong competition (think ahead when planting); in winter, protect from dampness and excessively strong sunlight
Arrangement: Looks nice with shades of yellow and pink (e.g., *Achillea, Asphodeline, Aster linosyris, Dianthus, Euphorbia cyparissias, Inula ensifolia, Sedum,* and *Thymus*)
Species/Varieties: Nanum Album (10 in./25 cm, white), Nanum Saphir (10 in./25 cm, blue); Narbonne Flax, *L. narbonense* (larger flowers), Six Hills variety (16 in./40 cm, violet); Golden Flax, *L. flavum* (12 in./30 cm, yellow flowers, May–July), Compactum variety

Height:
*8–12 inches/
20–30 cm*
**Blooming
Time:**
April–June

Lithospermum purpureocaeruleum

Cheddar Wood
Also Known as: Purple Gromwell, Purple Puccoon

Family: Borage plants *(Boraginaceae)*
Native to: Europe, Turkey, Syria, Caucasus, Northern Iran
Bloom: Gentian blue flowers; later on, white fruits appear
Appearance: Gray-green, lanceolate, slightly hairy leaves; the plant spreads by means of its long, above-ground runners; needs a little time to get started
Location: Sun to partial shade; for warm, dry places; likes lime; also grows in the shade, but not as sumptuously, and doesn't flower in the shade
Planting: Best in the spring
Care: Cut back in the fall
Arrangement: Fits in along the edge of wooded areas (e.g., with *Clematis* × *jouiniana, Corydalis, Digitalis, Geranium,* and with grasses)
Species/Varieties: Related species: Comfrey, *Symphytum grandiflorum* (12 in./30 cm, cream-white, March–May), Goldsmith (cream white, yellow variegated leaves), Hidcote Blue (light blue), Hidcote Pink (soft pink)

Height:
24–32 inches/ 60–80 cm
Blooming Time:
July–Sept.

Lobelia siphilitica

Great Blue Lobelia

Family: Bellflower plants *(Campanulaceae)*
Native to: USA
Bloom: Blue flowers in heads
Appearance: Bushy growth; flower stems have leaves all the way to the top; narrow, oval, ciliate leaves
Location: Sun (but not hot) to partial shade; moist to damp ground rich in nutrients, but with no standing water
Planting: Can be planted from spring to fall
Care: Don't let the ground dry out
Arrangement: Goes well with nearly all colors; attractive with *Bistorta, Eupatorium, Filipendula, Lysimachia,* and *Veronicastrum*
Notes: Good for cutting; the whole plant is poisonous
Species/Varieties: Blaue Auslese; *L. × speciosa:* Fan series (24 in./60 cm, erect flower spikes in red, violet, pink, and white, July–Sept.), Compliment Series (32 in./80 cm, blooms red or pink); *Lobelia × gerardii* (35–39 in./90–100 cm, Aug.–Sept., long-lasting), Rosenkavalier variety (dark pink); *Lobelia* hybrid Eulalia Berridge (35 in./90 cm, raspberry-red and pink)

Height:
*32–39 inches/
80–100 cm*
**Blooming
Time:**
June–July

Lupinus Hybrids

Lupine

Family: Leguminosae *(Fabaceae)*
Bloom: Spikes in blue, red, pink, yellow, or white; often bicolor
Appearance: Bushy growth; finger-shaped, compound, dark-green leaves; rigid, erect flower stems
Location: Sun to partial shade; porous, fairly damp and slightly sour soils, especially in the spring
Planting: Prefers spring planting
Care: Significant cutting back after flowering encourages new leaves to sprout, and sometimes a second blooming
Arrangement: Leaves empty spaces after flowering, so plant only in small groups and combine with neighbors that are attractive later on, such as *Achillea, Paeonia, Papaver,* and *Phlox*
Species/Varieties: My Castle (brick red, → illus.), Castellan (blue), Kronleuchter (yellow); similar: False Indigo, *Baptisia australis* (32–47 in./80–120 cm, blue flower candles, June–Aug., attractive black seedpods, long-lasting foliage)

Height:
*24–32 inches/
60–80 cm*
**Blooming
Time:**
June–Aug.

Lysimachia ciliata 'Firecracker'

Purple-leaved Loosestrife

Family: Primrose plants *(Primulaceae)*
Native to: Canada, USA
Bloom: Small, light yellow flowers in erect spikes
Appearance: Erect stems covered with leaves until flowering;
red-brown, lanceolate leaves; forms runners
Location: Sun; moist to damp soils rich in nutrients
Planting: Can be planted from spring to fall
Care: Water during prolonged drought
Arrangement: Showy leaf color; goes well with other red-
leafed species, with white and yellow flowers such as *Achillea,
Anthemis, Coreopsis, Ageratina* Chocolate, *Geranium, Phlox
maculata, Pseudolysimachion, Thalictrum,* and *Trollius*
Notes: The blooms are good for cutting.
Species/Varieties: *L. punctata* (24–35 in./60–90 cm, small
yellow flowers in erect panicles, June–Aug., spreads out, easy
to care for), Alexander (24 in./60 cm, yellow, green-white
leaves, for partial shade), Hometown Hero (32 in./80 cm,
deep yellow, does not proliferate)

Height:
*32 inches/
80 cm*
**Blooming
Time:**
July–Sept.

Lysimachia clethroides

Gooseneck Loosestrife ✿
Also Known as: Shepherd's Crook

Family: Primrose plants *(Primulaceae)*
Native to: China, Japan, Indochina
Bloom: Small, white flowers in candles bend horizontally
Appearance: Erect stems with leaves all the way up to the bloom; pointed, fairly long, oval leaves; attractive orange-red fall coloring; likes to form runners and spread out
Location: Sun to partial shade; moist to damp soils rich in nutrients; likes to be near water
Planting: Can be planted from spring to fall
Care: Water during prolonged drought
Arrangement: Goes with all colors; attractive when planted several together in narrow strips; good neighbors include *Bistorta, Chelone, Geranium, Lythrum, Monarda,* and *Vernonia*
Species/Varieties: Snowcandle hybrid (Aug.–Sept., compact growth); similar: *L. ephemerum* (32 in./80 cm, narrow, erect panicles in white, July–Aug.)

Height:
*24–59 inches/
60–150 cm*
**Blooming
Time:**
July–Sept.

Lythrum salicaria

European Purple Loosestrife ✿

Family: Loosestrife plants *(Lythraceae)*
Native to: Europe, Himalayas, Japan, Northern Africa, Australia
Bloom: Slender, erect flower spikes in red and pink
Appearance: Clustered growth; stems seem woody; narrow, lanceolate leaves up to the branched inflorescence; after flowering, they look quite disorderly
Location: Sun; moist to damp soils; likes to be near water; also tolerates partial shade, short periods of drought, and temporary waterlogging
Planting: Can be planted from spring to fall
Care: Remove blooms that have gone by to avoid self-seeding.
Arrangement: Attractive with blue, white, and red or pink plants such as *Aconitum, Cimicifuga, Eupatorium, Filipendula, Leucanthemella, Lysimachia, Phlox maculata,* and *Tradescantia.*
Species/Varieties: Blush (32–39 in./80–100 cm, light pink, double), The Rocket (59 in./150 cm, red-pink), Robert (32 in./80 cm, salmon-pink), Stichflamme (47 in./120 cm, large flowers, red), Gypsy Blood (47 in./120 cm, deep red); *L. virgatum* (24 in./60 cm, showy), Rose Queen variety (pink)

Height:
*16–24 inches/
40–60 cm*
**Blooming
Time:**
June–Sept.

Malva moschata

Musk Mallow

Family: Mallow plants *(Malvaceae)*
Native to: Europe, Western Turkey, North America
Bloom: Light pink or white, funnel-shaped flowers in small bunches on branched stems
Appearance: More or less erect growth; pronounced digitate green leaves; often short-lived
Location: Sunny and warm; moderately dry to moist soils rich in nutrients; also out of the sun
Planting: Can be planted from spring to fall
Care: To prevent going to seed, cut back after flowering
Arrangement: Goes with *Anaphlis, Bistorta, Centaurea dealbata, Lavandula, Nepeta, Papaver, Saponaria officinalis,* and *Solidago*
Notes: The flowers have a delicate aroma like musk.
Species/Varieties: Alba (white); Common Mallow, *M. silvestris* (up to 59 in./150 cm, purple with dark veins, July–Oct., often only annual, seeds itself); Oregon Checkerbloom, *Sidalcea oregana* July–Sept., Brilliant (28 in./70 cm, carmine red), My Love (35 in./90 cm, pink), Party Girl (39 in./100 cm, purple-red)

Height:
28–59 inches/
70–150 cm
**Blooming
Time:**
June–Aug.

Monarda Hybrids

Bee Balm Scarlet

Family: Mint family *(Lamiaceae)*
Bloom: White, red, pink, or purple lipped flowers arranged like a bouquet around the center
Appearance: Erect clusters that spread irregularly by means of short runners; small toothed leaves
Location: Sun to partial shade; moist to damp soils rich in nutrients (but no standing moisture)
Planting: Can be planted from spring to fall
Care: Cutting back after the first flowering helps combat mildew; also, attractive seedpods form from the flower whorls. Some varieties must be divided every year.
Arrangement: Not suited to cover large areas; companions are *Aster, Cimicifuga, Eupatorium, Nepeta sibirica,* and *Rudbeckia*
Notes: The leaves have an aromatic scent; for the vase, cut flowers as they open up.
Species/Varieties: Gardenview Scarlet (red, → illus.), Beauty of Cobham (pink-purple), Croftway Pink (pink), Mrs. Perry (light red), Prairie Night (purple), Scorpion (violet)

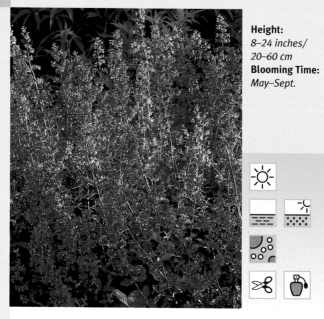

Height:
*8–24 inches/
20–60 cm*
Blooming Time:
May–Sept.

Nepeta × faassenii

Blue Catmint ✿

Family: Mint family *(Lamiaceae)*
Bloom: Small, blue or violet lipped flowers in small panicles on frequently low-lying flower shoots
Appearance: Clustered, bushy growth; small, oval, slightly toothed, gray-green leaves
Location: Full sun, warm locations; undemanding; thrives even on poor soils, but preferably on moderately dry, sandy-loamy soils
Planting: Can be planted from spring to fall.
Care: Cutting back encourages a second flowering.
Arrangement: Lower varieties are good for edging; attractive partners are *Allium, Anaphalis, Aster, Coreopsis, Geranium, Gypsophila, Iris barbata, Oenothera, Rudbeckia,* and *Sedum*
Notes: The leaves have an aromatic fragrance.
Species/Varieties: Walker's Low (24 in./60 cm, dark violet, → illus.), Blauknirps (8 in./20 cm, blue), Six Hills Giant (16–20 in./40–50 cm, purple), Snowflake (12 in./30 cm, white); *N. citriodora* (12 in./30 cm, purple flower, May–Aug., the leaves smell like lemon)

Height:
*28–35 inches/
70–90 cm*
**Blooming
Time:**
July–Sept.

Nepeta sibirica

Siberian Catmint

Family: Mint family *(Lamiaceae)*
Native to: Siberia, Mongolia, China
Bloom: Blue lipped flowers in loose, erect panicles
Appearance: Clustered growth; green leaves, pointed and lanceolate, slightly toothed; with occasional runners
Location: Sunny and warm; prefers moist soils and keeping its foot in the shade
Planting: Can be planted from spring to fall
Care: Cut back after blooming
Arrangement: Attractive with yellow, pink, or white (e.g., *Aster, Campanula, Gysophila, Oenothera, Physostegia,* and *Solidago*)
Notes: The blooms are good for cutting.
Species/Varieties: Souvenir d'André Chaudron (35 in./90 cm, blue-purple); Giant Catmint, *N. grandiflora* (35 in./80 cm, June–Sept.), Dawn to Dusk variety (soft pink); Catmint, *N. nervosa* (12–20 in./30–50 cm, light blue flowers, July–Aug., gray-green leaves); *N. subsessilis* 12–35 in./30–90 cm, thick, violet-blue flower whorls, July–Sept., nettle-like leaf)

Height:
*16–24 inches /
40 60 cm*
**Blooming
Time:**
June–Sept.

Oenothera fruticosa

Narrow-leaf Evening Primrose
Also Known as: Sundrops; Oenothera tetragona

Family: Willow Herb or Evening Primrose family *(Onagraceae)*
Native to: USA, Mexico
Bloom: Large, yellow flower bowls in bunches
Appearance: Erect shoots; leaf rosettes appear in the fall and remain over the winter; at blooming time, they produce the long flower stem leaves all the way to the top
Location: Sun; porous soils rich in nutrients; fairly moist, but also tolerates temporary drought
Planting: Can be planted from spring to fall
Care: Remove wilted parts; protect from winter dampness
Arrangement: Particularly attractive with blue and violet (e.g., *Aster, Nepeta, Pseudolysimachion,* and *Salvia*)
Species/Varieties: Sundrops (large flowers, reddish leaves, → illus.), Erica Robin (leaf rosettes mottled pink-yellow over winter); *O. macrocarpa* (6–8 in./15–20 cm, light yellow flowers on low shoots, winged fruits, June–Sept.), Greencourt Lemon variety (lemon yellow, gray-green leaves)

Height:
*6 inches/
15 cm*
**Blooming
Time:**
March–May

Omphalodes verna

Creeping Forget-Me-Not ✿
Also Known as: Blue-eyed Mary

Family: Borage or Forget-Me-Not *(Boraginaceae)*
Native to: Southern, Eastern, and Central Europe
Bloom: Small, bright blue or white flowers similar to Forget-Me-Not, in loose bunches
Appearance: Carpet-like growth; long oval, rough bunches of leaves in light green; spreads through runners
Location: For partial shade to deep shade; moist to dry soils rich in nutrients; doesn't like falling leaves
Planting: Can be planted from spring to fall
Care: Cover with humus in winter/spring
Arrangement: Good early bloomer that still looks appropriate later in the year; goes well with *Astilbe, Convallaria, Dicentra, Epimedium, Helleborus, Primula,* and *Tiarella*
Species/Varieties: Alba (white, slow growing), Grandiflora (blue, large-flowered); Navelwort, *O. cappadocica* Cherry Ingram (bright blue) and Starry Eyes (10 in./25 cm, light blue flowers with white rim, April–May, also tolerates sun; threatened by frost in cold areas)

Height:
*16 inches/
40 cm*
**Blooming
Time:**
July–Sept.

Origanum laevigatum

Purple Oregano

Family: Mint family *(Lamiaceae)*
Native to: Turkey, Cyprus
Bloom: Small, pink or red-violet lipped flowers in umbels
Appearance: Clustered growth; stems not always sturdy; small, dark green, oval leaves
Location: Full sun; warm and dry climate; likes lime
Planting: Can be planted from spring to fall
Care: Cut back the old shoots in the fall
Arrangement: Plant in groups; goes with *Achillea, Allium, Anaphalis, Artemisia schmidtiana* Nana, *Calamintha, Gypsophila, Lavandula, Platycodon, Salvia, Sedum,* and *Stachy*
Notes: Has a slight aroma of marjoram
Species/Varieties: Herrenhausen (16 in./40 cm, red-violet, dark foliage, less fragrant), Hopley's (24 in./60 cm, purple-pink), Rosenkuppel (16 in./40 cm, reddish green foliage); Oregano, *O. vulgare* (6–16 in./15–40 cm, July–Sept., strongly scented), Country Cream (12 in./30 cm, purple-pink, white-mottled leaves), Thumbles Variety (8 in./20 cm, purple, yellow foliage, partial shade)

Height:
32–47 inches/ 80–120 cm
Blooming Time:
June

Paeonia lactiflora

Chinese Peony

Family: Peony family *(Paeoniaceae)*
Native to: East Siberia, China, Tibet, Korea
Bloom: Large, single to largely double flower balls in white, pink, and red and on stems that are not always sturdy
Appearance: Clustered, not always sturdy growth; attractive, large leaf that lasts until fall
Location: Sun; loamy soils rich in nutrients
Planting: In fall, the eyes should be only about an inch (2–3 cm) underground; doesn't like being transplanted
Care: Cut away leaves in fall, for they are needed for forming new eyes; provide support if necessary
Arrangement: Specimen plant; becomes increasingly luxurious with age; attractive with *Anaphalis, Aster, Delphinium, Gypsophila, Hemerocallis, Iris, Lupinus, Nepeta,* and *Salvia*
Notes: Flowers for cutting; many varieties have a delicate aroma
Species/Varieties: Countless varieties and hybrids, for example, La Perle (light pink), Marie Lemoine (white), Sarah Bernhardt (pink, fragrant); Common Peony, *P. officinalis* (blooms earlier)

Height:
*28–39 inches/
70–100 cm*
**Blooming
Time:**
May–July

Papaver orientale

Oriental Poppy

Family: Poppy Family *(Papaveraceae)*
Native to: Turkey, Caucasus, Northern Iran
Bloom: Large bowl-shaped flowers in bright red, pink, or
white, usually dark-spotted flower base, partially fringed
flower petals; attractive caps for fruit pods
Appearance: Large, roughly haired leaves, fairly long and
incised; draws in after flowering, but new bunches of leaves
grow until fall
Location: Full sun and warm; tolerates no standing moisture
Planting: Difficult to transplant because of the long taproot
Care: Cut back after blooming
Arrangement: Use only individually or in small groups, for
after blooming they leave gaps; goes with *Lavandula, Leucanthemum, Delphinium, Iris barbata, Lupinus,* and *Salvia*
Species/Varieties: Numerous varieties, for example, Ali Baba
(red, → illus.), Patty's Plum (plum colors), Perry's White (white
with dark spots); Iceland poppy, *P. nudicale* (12 in./30 cm,
shades of white, yellow, orange, and red, short-lived, self-seeding)

Height:
*12–39 inches/
30–100 cm*
Blooming Time:
July–Sept.

Penstemon Hybrids

Penstemon
Also Known as: Heller's Beard Tongue

Family: Leadwort family *(Scrophulariaceae)*
Bloom: White, pink, or purple figwort flowers in loose panicles
Appearance: Erect, leafy flower stems; lanceolate leaves in rosettes close to the ground
Location: Full sun and warm; porous soil
Planting: Prefers spring planting
Care: Not dependably frost-resistant; protect in winter
Arrangement: Attractive with blue, violet; appropriate neighbors for the blue-purple varieties are *Achillea, Bergenia, Calamintha, Coreopsis, Nepeta, Phlox maculata,* and *Salvia*
Notes: The blooms are good for cutting.
Species/Varieties: Many varieties: Catherine de la Mere (24 in./60 cm, blue-violet, dark green leaves), Penstemon Ruby (24 in./60 cm, scarlet red), Snowstorm (20 in./50 cm, white), Sour Grapes (20 in./50 cm, blue), Züriblau (12 in./30 cm, blue); Beard Tongue, *P. barbatus* (32 in./80 cm, pink to purple-red, June–Aug.); Foxglove Penstemon, *P. digitalis* Husker's Red (24–39 in./60–100 cm, white, June–Aug., brown-colored foliage, very winter-hardy)

Height:
*20–39 inches/
50–100 cm*
**Blooming
Time:**
June–July

Phlomis russeliana

Jerusalem Sage   ✿

Family: Mint family *(Lamiaceae)*
Native to: Turkey, Southern Europe
Bloom: Yellow lipped flowers in thick, round whorls of several groups superimposed on one another on erect stems; the stalks remain attractive through the winter
Appearance: Loose to sturdy, erect growth; large, heart-shaped to pointed, oval leaves, covered with gray down
Location: Full sun; prefers porous and fairly dry soil but accepts any well-drained garden soil
Planting: Can be planted from spring to fall
Care: Cut off stalks in the spring; protect from winter dampness
Arrangement: Attractive structure even in winter; attractive with blue, violet, and dark red; appropriate neighboring plants include *Achillea, Asphodeline, Aster, Centranthus, Crambe, Echinops, Gypsophila, Iris, Nepeta, Redbeckia,* and *Salvia*
Species/Varieties: Similar: *P. samia* (lower), Green Glory variety; *P. tuberosa* (55 in./140 cm, pink-purple, May–June), Amazon variety

Height:
*12–16 inches/
30–40 cm*
**Blooming
Time:**
April–June

Phlox divaricata

Woodland Phlox

Family: Phlox family *(Polemoniaceae)*
Native to: Canada, USA
Bloom: Luxuriant flower carpet in shades of blue, purple, or white; individual flowers in cymes
Appearance: Loose, bushy growth; oval leaves
Location: Half shade to partial shade and cool; porous, sandy soils containing clay and rich in nutrients
Planting: Can be planted from spring to fall
Care: Protect from snails and slugs
Arrangement: Goes particularly well with white, yellow, and pink (e.g., *Euphorbia, Geranium, Helleborus,* and *Heuchera*), and with other blue flowers such as *Omphalodes* and *Platycodon*
Species/Varieties: Fuller's White (white, → illus.), Chattahoochee (violet, purple-red eye), Clouds of Perfume (blue-violet); for partial shade: *P. stolonifera* (10 in./25 cm, April–June, some runners, for slightly sour soils), Blue Ridge (blue), Home Fires (pink), Purpurea (bright purple)

137

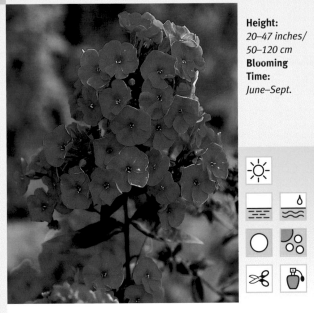

Height:
*20–47 inches/
50–120 cm*
**Blooming
Time:**
June–Sept.

Phlox paniculata

Garden Phlox

Family: Phlox family *(Polemoniaceae)*
Native to: USA
Bloom: Small blooms in thick panicles; shades of red, pink, and purple, plus white, sometimes two-colored
Appearance: Clustered growth with erect stems branched to the top; lanceolate, partly reddish leaves
Location: Sun; fairly damp soils rich in nutrients; better in partial shade on dry soils; likes to keep its feet cool
Planting: Can be planted from spring to fall
Care: Cut off wilted parts to encourage side buds to bloom; to lengthen or postpone the flowering time, shorten the shoots by a third at the start of June.
Arrangement: The panicles of flowers work well with Compositae such as *Aster, Erigeron, Helenium,* and *Leucanthemum*
Notes: Danger of mildew depends on location and weather. Many varieties smell aromatic, lemony, flowery.
Species/Varieties: Many varieties; *P. maculata* (showier, healthier, June–Sept.); *P. × arendsii* (20–24 in./50–60 cm, June–Aug.)

Height:
*20–39 inches/
50–100 cm*
**Blooming
Time:**
July–Sept.

Physalis alkekengi var. *franchetii*

Chinese Lantern Plant

Family: Nightshade family *(Solanaceae)*
Native to: Japan, Korea, Northern China
Bloom: Inconspicuous white flowers; the orange-red Lantern Plants are more impressive and attractive, and they produce fruits
Appearance: Erect growth; large, oval leaves that turn yellow in the fall; forms strong runners
Location: Sun to partial shade; moist to damp, porous soils; likes lime
Planting: Can be planted from spring to fall
Care: In restricted area, may build up rhizome block
Arrangement: Goes well at the edge of a wooded area, but needs neighbors to hold back its strong inclination to spread (e.g., *Artemisia, Eupatorium, Helenium, Hemerocallis, Lysimachia clethroides, L. punctata, Phlomis,* and grasses)
Notes: They are good for drying. The shoots are hung head-down.
Species/Varieties: Gigantea (39 in./100 cm, large, red fruits), Zwerg (8 in./20 cm, red-orange fruits)

Height:
24–47 inches/
60–120 cm
Blooming Time:
July–Sept.

Physostegia virginiana

False Dragonhead
Also Known as: Obedient Plant, Virginia Lion's Heart

Family: Mint family *(Lamiaceae)*
Native to: Canada, USA
Bloom: Erect flower heads consisting of individual, horizontal pink, red, or white flowers
Appearance: Erect, clumped growth; narrow, lanceolate summer-green leaves and angular stems
Location: Sun to light partial shade; moist to damp soils rich in nutrients, but not damp soils
Planting: Can be planted from spring to fall.
Care: Short-lived unless regularly divided and transplanted
Arrangement: Appropriate neighbors are blue, violet, and pink-red plants such as *Aster, Echinacea, Erigeron, Liatris, Monarda, Phlox, Pseudolysimachion,* and *Salvia*
Notes: Cut flowers for the vase as they bloom.
Species/Varieties: Vivid (pink, → illus.), Bouquet Rose (purple-pink), Van Wassehove (purple-pink), Red Beauty (red), Summer Spire (violet-red), Snow Crown, Summer Snow (white)

Height:
*16–20 inches/
40–50 cm*
**Blooming
Time:**
July–Aug.

Platycodon grandiflorus

Balloon Flower

Family: Bellflower plants *(Campanulaceae)*
Native to: Japan, North Korea, China
Bloom: Balloon-like buds that open into large flat, star-shaped bells, in blue, pink, or white
Appearance: Clustered; blue-green leaves; sprouts fairly late
Location: Sun to partial shade; porous soils very rich in nutrients; quite undemanding
Planting: Can be planted from spring to fall
Care: The plant may need to be staked
Arrangement: Empty spaces are the result of the late sprouting; can be filled with early bloomers; attractive with *Dianthus, Euphorbia, Helleborus, Omphalodes,* and *Geum*
Notes: The blooms are good for cutting
Species/Varieties: Album (20 in./50 cm, white); Astra series (8 in./20 cm, blue, white, or pink, also blue double), Blaue Glocke (28 in./70 cm, blue), Fuji series (20 in./50 cm, deep blue, white, pink), Mariesii (16 in./40 cm, blue), Perlmutterschale (20 in./50 cm, pink); Apoyama group (8–10 in./20–25 cm, varieties in white and purple–blue)

141

Height:
*16–28 inches/
40–70 cm*
**Blooming
Time:**
May–June

Polemonium caeruleum ssp. *caeruleum*

Jacob's Ladder
Also Known as: Ladder Polemonium

Family: Phlox plants *(Polemoniaceae)*
Native to: Europe, Turkey, Siberia
Bloom: Small, blue and/or white blooms in bunches
Appearance: Erect growth; attractive feathery leaf bunches, sometimes variegated; quite short-lived
Location: Sun, partial shade; moist to damp soil, containing humus
Planting: Can be planted from spring to fall
Care: With cutting back, will bloom a second time
Arrangement: Attractive spring bloomer; the blue varieties are particularly attractive with yellow (e.g., *Aquilegia, Doronicum, Euphorbia, Geum, Hemerocallis,* and *Trollius*)
Notes: The flowers have a sweet fragrance.
Species/Varieties: Album (white), Brise d'anjou (white-mottled leaf, cover in winter), Königssee (gentian blue); *P. reptans* (12–16 in./30–40 cm, April–May), Blue Pearl (blue), Lambrook Mauve (violet), Pink Beauty (purple-pink); *P. × richardsonii* (20 in./50 cm, sky blue, blooms until fall)

Height:
*24–39 inches/
60–100 cm*
**Blooming
Time:** *June*

Polygonatum × hybridum

Solomon's Seal ✿

Family: Lily of the Valley plants (*Convallariaceae*)
Native to: Europe, Turkey, Caucasus, Himalayas, Japan
Bloom: Small, white flowers lined up on overhanging stems;
later on, black-blue berries develop from the flowers
Appearance: Slender forms; fairly long, oval leaves in green,
sometimes also variegated; readily forms runners
Location: Partial to full shade; moist to moderately damp soils
rich in nutrients
Planting: Can be planted from spring to fall
Care: Avoid hoeing near roots
Arrangement: Plant in rows; attractive with *Alchemilla,
Astilbe, Geranium, Helleborus, Heuchera, Hosta, Omphalodes,*
and *Vinca*
Notes: All plant parts are slightly poisonous. Cut for the vase
when two-thirds of the panicles bloom.
Species/Varieties: Grace Barker (green-white, variegated
leaf), Variegatum (leaf with white margin), Striatum (white),
Weihenstephan (white, early bloomer)

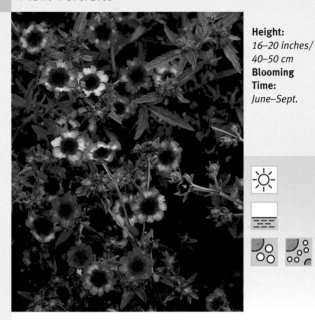

Height:
*16–20 inches/
40–50 cm*
**Blooming
Time:**
June–Sept.

Potentilla nepalensis

Nepal Cinquefoil ✿
Also Known as: Miss Willmott

Family: Rose plants *(Rosaceae)*
Native to: Western Himalayas
Bloom: Bowl-shaped, similar to strawberry, pink flowers
Appearance: Bushy; similar to strawberry, wintergreen leaves
Location: Full sun and warm; porous, moist to occasionally dry soils; otherwise undemanding
Planting: Can be planted from spring to fall
Care: Easy to care for
Arrangement: Good for flowerbed (e.g., with *Achillea, Aster, Lavandula, Nepeta, Origanum, Platycodon, Salvia,* and *Sedum*)
Species/Varieties: Miss Willmott (16 in./40 cm, carmine pink, → illus.), Ron McBeath (12 in./30 cm, carmine red), Roxana (16 in./40 cm, yellow-pink); further moderately tall species: *P. atrosanguinea* (16 in./40 cm, red, June–Aug., gray, downy leaves), Gibson's Scarlet (scarlet, green foliage); *P. thurberi* (12 in./30 cm, dark red, dark green leaf); *Potentilla* hybrid Etna (18 in./45 cm, velvety red, July–Sept., silvery leaves)

Height:
*4–6 inches/
10–15 cm*
**Blooming
Time:**
Feb.–April

Primula vulgaris

Common Primrose
Also Known as: English Primrose

Family: Primrose plants *(Primulaceae)*
Native to: Europe, Asia Minor
Bloom: Single to double flowers in bunches; partially wavy flower petals in practically all colors
Appearance: Basal leaf rosette; fairly long, oval, wrinkled; the flower stems grow from the rosettes
Location: Sun to partial shade and fairly cool; moist to damp soils containing humus
Planting: Plant in the spring.
Care: Water during drought.
Arrangement: Appropriate for the edge of wooded areas, with spring-blooming bulb plants, and with *Bellis* and *Mysotis*
Notes: The plant is mildly poisonous.
Species/Varieties: Usually not marketed in varieties. *P. ×
bullesiana* and *P. bulleyana* (16–20 in./40–50 cm, yellow, red, and orange, June–July); Himalayan Primrose, *P. denticulata* (12 in./30 cm, March–May); Oxlip, *P. elatior* and *P. veris* (10 or 6 in./25 or 15 cm, yellow, April–May)

Height:
*32 inches/
80 cm*
**Blooming
Time:**
July–Aug.

Pseudolysimachion longifolium

Longleaf Speedwell

Family: Leadwort plants *(Scrophlariaceae)*
Native to: Europe, Siberia, Central Asia, Caucasus
Bloom: Narrow flower spikes in blue, pink, or white
Appearance: Erect, clustered growth; branched stems
Location: Sunny and warm; moist to damp soils rich in nutrients; doesn't like locations with lots of lime
Planting: Can be planted from spring to fall
Care: Water during extended drought
Arrangement: The candle-shaped flowers work best with yellow or pink umbels or composite flowers. Good neighbors are thus *Achillea, Buphtalmum, Coreopsis,* and *Erigeron.*
Notes: The spikes are cut for the vase as they open up.
Species/Varieties: Blauriesin, Pink Damask, Schneeriesin; *P. spicatum* (depending on variety, 8–16 in./20–40 cm, blue or pink, July–Sept.); *Veronica gentianoides* (20 in./50 cm at blooming, otherwise flat, gentian-like leafy cushions, light blue, May–June)

Height:
*8–12 inches/
20–30 cm*
**Blooming
Time:**
March–May

Pulmonaria angustifolia

Blue Lungwort
Also Known as: Blue Cowslip

Family: Borage plants *(Boraginaceae)*
Native to: Europe (except for the Iberian Peninsula and the British Isles)
Bloom: Small, blue, funnel-shaped flowers in clusters
Appearance: Long, oval, hairy leaves that still look attractive after flowering; spreads through rhizomes
Location: Partial shade to shade; porous, moist soils containing humus and rich in nutrients
Planting: Can be planted from spring to fall
Care: Avoid hoeing near roots
Arrangement: Good spring bloomer; goes well with *Anemone nemorosa, Dicentra, Epimedium, Primula,* and *Waldsteinia*
Species/Varieties: Azurea (gentian blue, → illus.), Mawson (gentian blue), Munstead Blue (blue); *P. rubra* (12 in./30 cm, red, March–May); Red Start variety (red); Mrs. Moon Lungwort, *P. saccharata* (10–12 in./25–30 cm, clustered, mottled leaves), Dora Bielefeld (pink), Mrs. Moon (red), Pink Dawn (pink), Sissinghurst White (white, large-flowered)

147

Height:
*8–10 inches/
20–25 cm*
**Blooming
Time:**
March–May

Pulsatilla vulgaris

Pasque Flower

Family: Buttercup or Crowfoot plants *(Ranunculaceae)*
Native to: Europe, Baltic
Bloom: Large, slightly angled bellflowers in pink, red, or white; decorative, cottony seedpods
Appearance: Clustered growth; hairy, feathery leaves that recede after flowering
Location: Full sun; in fairly poor, moderately moist soils that contain lime and are dry in the summer
Planting: Prefers spring planting
Care: Fertilize little or not at all
Arrangement: Doesn't like any vigorous neighbors; goes well with *Dianthus, Iberis, Iris, Teucrium,* and *Thymus*
Notes: All plant parts are poisonous.
Species/Varieties: Alba (white), Papageno (mixture, some fringed flower petals), Red Bell (red), White Swam; for similar locations: Snowdrop Anemone, *Anemone sylvestris* (8–12 in./20–30 cm, white, mildly fragrant, bowl–shaped flowers, woolly seeds, hairy incised leaves, also in partial shade)

Height:
*35–59 inches/
80–150 cm*
**Blooming
Time:**
May–July

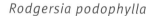

Rodgersia podophylla

Rodgersia

Family: Saxifrage plants *(Saxifragaceae)*
Native to: Japan, Korea
Bloom: Large, erect flower panicles in cream white
Appearance: Very large, hand-shaped, deeply incised leaves, sometimes reddish while growing and in the fall; spreads over time through rhizomes; develops slowly
Location: Partial to full shade; in soils rich in nutrients and moist, but without standing water
Planting: Can be planted from spring to fall
Care: Water during extended drought
Arrangement: Impressive leafy perennial, attractive with light-colored flowers (e.g., *Astilbe, Anemone, Aruncus, Cimicifuga,* and *Digitalis*)
Species/Varieties: Rotlaub (protruding panicles), Smaragd (cream white); *R. aesculifolia* (bronze-colored leaves similar to horse chestnut); *R. pinnata*: (hand-shaped leaves); similar: Table Leaf, *Astilboides tabularis* (saucer-shaped leaves, white, slightly overhanging flower panicles, July)

Height:
*24–32 inches/
60–80 cm*
**Blooming
Time:**
July–Sept.

Rudbeckia fulgida

Orange Coneflower ✿

Family: Compositae *(Asteraceae)*
Native to: USA
Bloom: Golden yellow, slightly pendent tongue flowers surrounding a dark brown, rounded center
Appearance: Sturdy, erect, clustered growth; dark green, rough, oval foliage decreasing in size above
Location: Sun; very undemanding as long as the soil is rich in nutrients and not too dry
Planting: Can be planted from spring to fall
Care: Water during prolonged drought
Arrangement: Goes well with blue, purple, and wine red (e.g., *Aster, Echinops, Erigeron, Helenium, Liatris,* and *Salvia*)
Notes: New growth is threatened by snails and slugs.
Species/Varieties: Goldsturm; *R. laciniata* (double, golden yellow flowers, Aug.–Oct., susceptible to snail and slug damage); Gold Ball (51 in./130 cm); Gold Fountain (24 in./ 60 cm); *R. nitida* (71–79 in./180–200 cm, yellow flowers, susceptible to snail and slug damage), Autumn Sun (Aug.– Sept.), July Gold (July–Aug.)

Height:
*16–28 inches/
40–70 cm*
**Blooming
Time:**
May–Sept.

Salvia nemorosa

May Night Sage

Family: Mint plants *(Lamiaceae)*
Bloom: Small lipped flowers in narrow panicles, various shades of blue, pink, and white; blooms twice
Appearance: Depending on variety, sturdy erect or broad, spreading, branched growth; rough, lanceolate leaves
Location: Sun; porous, moist to occasionally dry soils rich in nutrients
Planting: Can be planted from spring to fall
Care: Cut back as flowers go by to encourage second blooming.
Arrangement: The species looks very attractive with *Achillea, Centranthus, Coreopsis, Geum, Rudbeckia, Sedum,* and other yellow and red flowers.
Notes: The leaves and flowers have a tangy, spicy fragrance.
Species/Varieties: Varieties also classified as *S. × sylvestris* or *S. superba*; Blue Hill (see illus.), Dancer (violet), Caradonna (dark violet), Amethyst (pink), Rosakönigen (pink), Adrian (white); Meadow Clary, *S. pratensis* (20 in./50 cm, blue violet, June–Aug., loose, bulky growth)

Height:
*20 inches/
50 cm*
**Blooming
Time:**
June–Sept.

Salvia verticillata

Lilac Sage
Also Known as: Purple Rain

Family: Mint family *(Lamiaceae)*
Native to: Europe, North America, Middle East
Bloom: Small, violet lipped flowers in small panicles, in loose, superimposed whorls
Appearance: Erect, clustered growth; quite sturdy; silvery, hairy, notched leaves
Location: Sun; porous soils rich in nutrients
Planting: Can be planted from spring to fall
Care: Blooms longer if wilted flowers are continually removed
Arrangement: Particularly attractive with light yellow, and with *Geranium, Hemerocallis, Potentilla, Saponaria,* and *Sedum*
Notes: Blooms last a long time in the vase.
Species/Varieties: Purple Rain (blue-violet with pink-purple calyx, → illus.), Smoldering Torches (darker, grows erect), Alba (white); *S. glutinosa* (32–39 in./80–100 cm, yellow flowers, July–Aug., heart-shaped foliage, for light shade, strong aroma, good for cutting); *Salvia* hybrid Indigo Spires (39 in./100 cm, long, blue panicles, protect during winter)

Height:
*12 inches/
30 cm*
**Blooming
Time:**
July–Aug.

Santolina chamaecyparissus

Lavender Cotton

Family: Compositae *(Asteraceae)*
Native to: Southern Europe, Northern Africa
Bloom: Small, yellow, rounded leaves
Appearance: Silver gray, feathery leaves, wintergreen; rounded, compact growth
Location: Sunny and warm; porous and fairly dry soils, not too rich in nutrients
Planting: Can be planted from spring to fall
Care: Cutting back right after blooming or in late spring keeps the plant compact in cold regions, protect from frost and winter moisture
Arrangement: Attractive all year long, also for borders or corners; goes with *Allium, Bergenia, Iris,* and *Lavandula*
Notes: Aromatic leaves; good for shaping
Species/Varieties: *S. chamaecyparissus* ssp. *tomentosa* Edward Bowles (16 in./40 cm, cream-yellow, gray leaves); Green Santolina, *S. rosmarinifolia* (yellow, green, needle-shaped leaves); Lemon Queen, *S. pinnata* (light yellow, green foliage)

Height:
*10–16 inches/
25–40 cm*
**Blooming
Time:**
June–Sept.

Saponaria × lempergii 'Max Frei'

Soapwort ✿

Family: Pink or Carnation plants *(Caryophyllaceae)*
Bloom: Umbel-shaped inflorescences in pink; long blooming time
Appearance: Slightly overhanging growth; lanceolate leaves
Location: Sun; moderately dry to moist soils with good drainage that are not too rich in nutrients; particularly good in combination with rocks
Planting: Can be planted from spring to fall
Care: This species is easy to care for; may need to be cut back after blooming
Arrangement: This species is a good long-term, late bloomer for the tops of walls and flowerbed borders.
Notes: The flowers have a delicate fragrance.
Species/Varieties: Bouncing Bet, *S. officinalis*, Rosea Plena and Rubra Plena (pink and red, double, both 32 in./80 cm, propagate through runners, fragrant); Rock Soapwort, *S. ocymoides* (6–8 in./15–20 cm, pink, June–July, protruding growth, easily self-seeding, various varieties with pink and white flowers)

Height:
*24–32 inches/
60–80 cm*
**Blooming
Time:**
June–Sept.

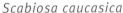

Scabiosa caucasica

Pincushion Flower
Also Known as: Butterfly Blue, Perfecta Blue

Family: Teasel plants *(Dipsacaceae)*
Native to: Caucasus
Bloom: Flat blue, violet, or white inflorescences
Appearance: Lanceolate basal leaves; slightly branched, loose, erect flower stems with feathery leaves
Location: Sun; porous soils containing humus and lime; sensitive to winter dampness
Planting: Best planted in the spring
Care: Divide every couple of years to keep the plant young
Arrangement: Goes well with yellow and white, such as *Achillea, Aster, Coreopsis, Erigeron, Liatris, Nepeta, Salvia,* and *Verbena*
Notes: A beautiful cut flower, but doesn't last long
Species/Varieties: Clive Greaves (sky blue, → illus.), Fama (deep lavender blue), Gudrun (violet, double), Compliment (light blue), Miss Willmott (white), Nachtfalter (dark purple), Perfecta Alba (cream white); Cream Pincushion, *S. ochroleuca* (24 in./60 cm, yellowish white, July–Sept., loose growth)

155

Height:
12–24 inches/
30 60 cm
Blooming
Time:
Aug.–Oct.

Sedum telephium

Stonecrop ✿
Also Known as: Witch's Moneybags, Autumn Joy

Family: Orpine plants *(Crassulaceae)*
Native to: Europe, Turkey, North America
Bloom: Thick, flat flower umbels in brown red, pink, or white; the inflorescences look attractive even in the winter
Appearance: Clustered growth; usually sturdy, erect stems with thick, fleshy partly reddish leaves all the way to the top
Location: Sun; porous, even poor soils not too rich in nutri-ents; also withstands lots of dryness
Planting: Can be planted from spring to fall
Care: Easy to care for; cut off old shoots in the spring
Arrangement: Well suited for edging; goes with *Achillea, Artemisia, Bergenia, Coreopsis, Geranium,* and *Nepeta*
Notes: Very long-lasting cut flowers
Species/Varieties: Matrona (light pink, reddish foliage, → illus.) and Autumn Joy (rust red) are 20–24 in./50–60 cm tall, Bertram Anderson (red, purple-red leaves), and Red Emperor (dark red foliage) are only 10 in./25 cm

Height:
*39–55 inches/
100–140 cm*
**Blooming
Time:**
July–Aug.

Silene chalcedonica

Burning Love
**Also Known as: Jerusalem Cross, Dusky Salmon,
Maltese Cross, Nonesuch**

Family: Pink or Carnation plants *(Caryophyllaceae)*
Native to: Russia, Northern China
Bloom: Gleaming red, pink, or white flowers in bunches
Appearance: Erect stems; lanceolate leaves; quite short-lived,
but self-seeding in appropriate locations
Location: Sun; otherwise very undemanding; prefers soils
with humus and not too much moisture
Planting: Water during periods of dryness
Care: Blooms a second time if cut back after flowering
Arrangement: Attractive with *Achillea, Buphtalmum, Del-
phinium, Leucanthemum, Lupinus, Nepeta, Phlox, Rudbeckia,*
and *Salvia*
Notes: The flowers are very good for cutting.
Species/Varieties: Alba (white), Carnea (dark pink), Rosea
(salmon pink); *S. arkwrightii* Vesuvius (16 in./40 cm, orange
red, May–June, dark foliage); Rose Compion, *S. coronaria*
(20–28 in./50–70 cm, carmine red, gray leaves), Alba (white);
Sticky Catchfly, *S. viscaria* (16–20 in./40–50 cm)

157

Height:
*20–32 inches/
50–80 cm*
**Blooming
Time:**
July–Sept.

Solidago Hybrids

Goldenrod ✿

Family: Compositae *(Asteraceae)*
Bloom: Small, yellow flowers in branched panicles
Appearance: Sturdy, erect growth; narrow, lanceolate leaves;
forms runners but doesn't run wild
Location: Sun, but also tolerates light shade; really unde-
manding; moist to damp soils
Planting: Can be planted from spring to fall
Care: Stake if necessary; cut off wilted flowers if self-seeding is
not desired; water during drought
Arrangement: Goes well in natural gardens and with *Aster,
Delphinium, Erigeron, Helenium, Heliopsis,* and *Rudbeckia*
Notes: Good flower for cutting
Species/Varieties: Golden Gate (20 in./50 cm), Goldenmosa
(28 in./70 cm, late blooming), Goldwedel (24 in./60 cm, early
bloomer), Ledsham (32 in./80 cm), Strahlenkrone (24 in./
60 cm, flat inflorescences, early bloomer); Blue Stemmed or
Wreath Goldenrod, *S. caesia* (20–24 in./50–60 cm, golden
yellow, Aug.–Oct., bluish stems); Common Goldenrod, *S.
vigaurea* Nana (16 in./40 cm)

Height:
*16–24 inches/
40–60 cm*
**Blooming
Time:**
May–July

Stachys macrantha

Big Betony
Also Known as: Stachys Grandiflora, Big Sage

Family: Mint family *(Lamiaceae)*
Native to: Turkey, Caucasus, Iran
Bloom: Pink-purple flower whorls on erect stems
Appearance: Gray-green, oval, notched foliage
Location: Sun to partial shade; moist to damp soils containing humus; even grown on poor soils
Planting: Can be planted from spring to fall
Care: Water during extended drought
Arrangement: Appropriate for perennial flowerbed and at the edges of wooded areas; attractive with light yellow and pur-ple-pink, (e.g., *Alchemilla, Allium, Bergenia, Calamintha, Coreopsis, Geum,* and *Hemerocallis*)
Notes: The blooms are good for cutting.
Species/Varieties: Superba (purple-pink); S. *monnieri* (June–July, attractive even after blooming), Hummelo (pur-ple), Rosea (pink); Common Hedgenettle, S. *officinalis* (24 in./60 cm, pink); Wooly Betony or Lamb's Ear, S. *byzantina* (8–12 in./20–30 cm, white felt-like leaves, for porous soils)

Height:
*12–16 inches/
30–40 cm*
**Blooming
Time:**
May–June

Tellima grandiflora

Fringe Cups ✿
Also Known as: False Alum Root

Family: Saxifrage plants *(Saxifragaceae)*
Native to: Alaska, Canada, USA
Bloom: Greenish, fairly inconspicuous bellflowers
Appearance: Rounded to heart-shaped, hairy leaf clusters
from which the delicate flower stems rise; wintergreen
Location: Partial to full shade; also suited to dry and damp
locations
Planting: Can be planted from spring to fall
Care: Avoid hoeing around roots
Arrangement: Attractive for planting under wooded areas and
with *Alchemilla, Astilbe, Heuchera, Pulmonaria,* and *Trollius*
Notes: Some varieties have a strong fragrance
Species/Varieties: Forest Frost (pink), Rubra (reddish foliage
in fall); *T. grandiflora* Odorata group (green flowers, strong
fragrance); × *Heucherella tiarelloides* (cross between *Heuchera*
and *Tiarella,* 16–20 in./40–50 cm, pink flowers, May–July,
heart-shaped flowers, forms runners)

Height:
*8–10 inches/
10–25 cm*
**Blooming
Time:**
June–July

Teucrium chamaedrys

Germander

Family: Mint family *(Lamiaceae)*
Native to: Europe, Turkey, Caucasus
Bloom: Small, purple-pink, lipped flowers in erect heads
Appearance: Brushy growth; small, oval, evergreen leaves; sometimes forms runners
Location: Sunny and warm; porous and fairly dry soils
Planting: Can be planted from spring to fall
Care: Protect from winter dampness
Arrangement: Suited for borders and can be trimmed into a low hedge but, then it doesn't bloom; attractive with *Achillea, Artemisia, Calamintha, Limonium, Nepeta, Oenothera, Origanum,* and *Santolina*
Species/Varieties: Nanum (8–10 in./10–15 cm, purple); Caucasus Germander, *T. hircanicum* (16–20 in./40–50 cm, purple-red, erect flower spikes, good for cutting, Aug.–Sept., dark green, fragrant foliage, spreads through runners)

Height:
*39–47 inches/
100–120 cm*
**Blooming
Time:**
May–July

Thalictrum aquilegifolium

Meadow Rue ❀

Family: Buttercup or Crowfoot plants (*Ranunculaceae*)
Native to: Europe (mainland), Northwestern Turkey
Bloom: Small, feathery, purple or white flowers in loose, feathery appearing panicles
Appearance: Erect, showy growth; foliage similar to Columbine
Location: Sun to partial shade; moist to damp, porous soils, but also tolerates temporary drought
Planting: Can be planted from spring to fall
Care: Water during prolonged drought
Arrangement: Showy structure, goes well with large flowers (e.g., *Aconitum, Astilbe, Campanula, Echinacea, Hemerocallis, Iris sibirica, Lythrum, Monarda, Trollius,* and *Veronicastrum*)
Notes: Bloom is good for cutting.
Species/Varieties: Album (white), Purpureum (purple), Thundercloud (purple); Meadow Rue, *T. dipterocarpum* (= *T. delavayi*; 47 in./120 cm, pink-purple, July–Sept., likes slightly acidic soils); Yellow Meadow Rue, *T. flavum* ssp. *glaucum* (71–79 in./180–200 cm, yellow flowers, June–July)

Height:
*6–8 inches/
15–20 cm*
**Blooming
Time:**
April–May

Tiarella cordifolia

Foamflower ✿

Family: Saxifrage plants *(Saxifragaceae)*
Native to: Canada, USA
Bloom: Soft, cream-white flower spikes
Appearance: Heart-shaped, wintergreen foliage, sometimes
with dark venation and copper-red colors in autumn
Location: Partial to full shade; prefers slightly acidic, damp,
humusy, loose soils; readily spreads through runners; doesn't
like winter dampness
Planting: Can be planted from spring to fall
Care: Avoid hoeing near roots
Arrangement: Appropriate for edge of flowerbed, for example,
with *Bergenia, Dicentra, Epimedium, Omphalodes, Primula,*
and *Pulmonaria*
Species/Varieties: Moorgrün (light green leaves, → illus.),
Moorblut (leaves with dark veins), Oakleaf (foliage similar
to oak), Rosalie (pink flowers), Simsalbim (white); similar:
T. wherryi (12 in./30 cm, cream-white flowers, May–June,
attractive foliage, no runners), Bronze Beauty variety
(red leaf)

Height:
*16–32 inches/
40–80 cm*
**Blooming
Time:**
June–Sept.

Tradescantia × andersoniana

Spiderwort

Family: Spiderwort plants *(Commelinaceae)*
Bloom: Three-part flower umbels in white, pink, red, and blue; individual flowers last only a short time, but new ones continually appear.
Appearance: Grass-like leaves that lasts a long time; reblooms reliably
Location: Sun to partial shade; humusy, loamy, moist to damp soils rich in nutrients; suffers during drought; likes water
Planting: Prefers spring planting.
Care: Cut back after first flowering so it will rebloom; this also keeps the plant from seeding itself; water during drought.
Arrangement: With *Astilbe, Bergenia, Epimedium, Filipendula, Hemerocallis, Hosta, Iris sibirica, Lythrum,* and *Lysimachia*
Notes: New growth is threatened by snails and slugs.
Species/Varieties: Bilberry Ice (white, blue eye), Blue Stone (gentian blue), Concord Grape (violet), Karminglut (carmine), Leonora (dark purple), Red Grape (red flowers, gray-green foliage), Zwanenburg Blue (dark blue)

Height:
*20 inches/
50 cm*
**Blooming
Time:**
Aug.–Sept.

Tricyrtis hirta

Hairy Toad Lily

Family: Lily of the Valley plants (*Convallariaceae*)
Native to: Japan
Bloom: The white-purple, red mottled flowers look like orchids.
Appearance: Erect growth; oval, dark green leaves; with some runners
Location: Half-shady to shady; fairly acidic soils that are rich in nutrients, damp, and cool
Planting: Prefers spring planting.
Care: Best to cover in winter
Arrangement: Doesn't like excessively vigorous neighbors; goes well with *Anemone hupehensis, Epimedium, Eupatorium, Heuchera, Hosta, Primula, Tiarella*, and *Waldsteinia*
Species/Varieties: *T. hirta* hybrid Miyazaki (32 in./80 cm, white purple, rich blooms); Taiwanese Toad Lily, *T. formosana* (32 in./80 cm, white with dark spots), Stolonifera Group (32 in./80 cm, red, mottled flowers, Aug.–Sept., dark foliate); *Tricyrtis* hybrids: Taiwan Adbane (20 in./50 cm, purple-red with dark spots) and Weisse Taube (20 in./50 cm, white)

Height:
*20–32 inches/
50–80 cm*
**Blooming
Time:**
April–July

Trollius × cultorum

Garden Globeflower
Also Known as: Golden Queen

Family: Buttercup or Crowfoot plants *(Ranunculaceae)*
Bloom: Spherical flowers in yellow, orange, and white
Appearance: Erect, clustered growth; summer green leaves
Location: Sun to partial shade; moist to damp, loamy soils
rich in nutrients; likes to be near water
Planting: Can be planted from spring to fall
Care: Cutting back after the first flowering produces a second
blooming (less robust); water during periods of drought
Arrangement: Attractive with blue flowers such as *Anchusa,
Brunnera, Campanula, Geranium, Hosta,* and *Iris sibirica*
Notes: All plant parts are poisonous
Species/Varieties: Alabaster (cream-white, late blooming),
Earliest of All (golden yellow, early blooming), Goldquelle
(golden yellow), Helios (lemon yellow), Lemon Queen
(lemon yellow), Orange Globe (orange); Chinese Globeflower,
T. chinensis (32–39 in./80–100 cm, orange-yellow, bowl-
shaped flowers, June–July)

Height:
*59–79 inches/
150–200 cm*
**Blooming
Time:**
June–Aug.

Verbascum bombyciferum

Giant Silver Mullein
Also Known as: Polar Summer

Family: Leadwort plants *(Scrophulariaceae)*
Bloom: Thick, erect panicles in yellow
Appearance: Basal rosette; erect, slightly branched flower stems; oval, gray fuzzy leaves; usually biennial
Location: Sunny and warm, but also likes heat; dry, porous, nutrient-poor soils
Planting: Self-seeding in appropriate locations
Care: Remove wilted blooms to foster vitality
Arrangement: The gray leaves harmonize with blue flowers (e.g., *Eryngium, Nepeta, Pseudolysimachion,* and *Salvia*).
Species/Varieties: *V. chaixii* (47–49 in./120–150 cm, yellow or white, July–Aug., green foliage); *Verbascum* hybrids (24–39 in./60–100 cm, May–Sept., sometimes with gray leaves), Jackie (16 in./40 cm, pink, dark eye, June–Sept.), Pink Domino (39 in./100 cm, purple-pink, May–June, long-lived), Royal Highland (28 in./70 cm, dark pink, May–June); *V. phoeniceum* (20–32 in./50–80 cm, white or violet, May–June, green leaves)

Height:
*59–63 inches/
150–160 cm*
**Blooming
Time:**
Aug.–Oct.

Vernonia arkansana

Arkansas Ironweed
Also Known as: Ozark Ironweed

Family: Compositae *(Asteraceae)*
Native to: USA
Bloom: Small, purple violet blooms in umbels
Appearance: Erect, clustered, usually sturdy growth; long, oval, rough, hairy leaves
Location: Sunny and warm; sufficiently moist to damp soils rich in nutrients; also tolerates brief drought and light partial shade; likes to be near water
Planting: Best planted in the spring
Care: Water during extended drought; the seedpods can remain over the winter
Arrangement: Solitary or at the most in small groups with *Aster, Boltonia, Chelone, Eupatorium, Helianthus, Leucanthemella, Ligularia, Rudbeckia, Solidago,* and grasses such as *Miscanthus, Molinia,* and *Panicum*
Notes: Cut the flowers for the vase as they appear.
Species/Varieties: Mammoth (87 in./220 cm, red-violet)

Height:
*39–63 inches/
100–160 cm*
**Blooming
Time:**
July–Sept.

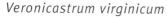

Veronicastrum virginicum

Culver's Root
Also Known as: Bowman's Root, Blackroot

Family: Leadwort plants *(Scrophulariaceae)*
Native to: Canada, USA
Bloom: Branched, candle-shaped inflorescences in blue, white, or pink (purple) on sturdy, erect stems; elegant effect
Appearance: Clustered growth; the long, oval leaves are arranged in whorls around the stem; quite sturdy
Location: Sun to partial shade; moist to damp soils rich in nutrients; also tolerates temporary drought
Planting: Can be planted from spring to fall
Care: Water during persistent drought
Arrangement: Solitary or in small groups with *Aster laevis, Baptisia, Bistorta, Boltonia, Coreopsis, Oenothera fructicosa, Phlox maculata, Rudbeckia,* and *Solidago*
Notes: Cut the spikes for the vase as they bloom.
Species/Varieties: Roseum (63 in./160 cm), Albo-Roseum (59 in./150 cm, soft pink, → illus.), Pink Glow (39 in./ 100 cm, light pink), Lavender Towers (47–55 in./120–140 cm, pink-purple), Fascination (55–63 in./140–160 cm, violet)

Height:
*4–6 inches/
10–15 cm*
**Blooming
Time:**
April–June

Vinca minor

Common Periwinkle ✿

Family: Dogbane plants *(Apocynaceae)*
Native to: Europe (mainland), Caucasus, Iran, Western Turkey
Bloom: Blue, red, or white blooms on creeping shoots
Appearance: Ground-covering growth; evergreen, sometimes variegated, oval leaves that may become frozen back in the winter
Location: Partial shade to deep shade; prefers moist to damp soils, but also grows in dry shade
Planting: Can be planted from spring to fall
Care: Very undemanding and easy to care for
Arrangement: This species is well suited for planting under wooded areas and for greening up shady slopes
Notes: The entire plant is poisonous.
Species/Varieties: Bowles Variety (blue, large flowers, → illus.), Variegata (blue, white mottled leaves), Atropurpurea (red-violet), Rubra (purple-red), Gertrude Jekyll (white, sumptuous blooms); Big Leaf Periwinkle, *V. major* (8–10 in./20–25 cm, larger leaves and blue flowers, sometimes white or yellow variegated leaves)

Height:
*6–12 inches/
15–30 cm*
**Blooming
Time:**
May–Oct.

Viola cornuta

Tufted Pansy
Also Known as: Horned Violet, Tufted Violet

Family: Violet plants *(Violaceae)*
Native to: Southern Europe
Bloom: Small to fairly large flowers resembling *Viola wittrock-iana* in all colors, sometimes multicolored with an eye
Appearance: Small, initially compact bunches that later separate from one another; wintergreen
Location: Sun to partial shade; humusy soils
Planting: Spring planting suits it best
Care: Cut back significantly after first flowering
Arrangement: Goes with other spring bloomers as well as with *Dianthus, Geum, Heuchera, Lamium,* and *Saponaria*
Species/Varieties: Winter-hardy varieties include Columbine
(→ illus.), Jackanapes (golden yellow with brown edge),
Molly Sanderson (black); Sweet Violet, *V. odorata* (4–6 in./
10–15 cm, March–April, fragrant, for shady locations),
Queen Charlotte (blue-violet); Common Blue Violet,
V. sororia (6 in./15 cm, May–June, summer green), Freckles
(blue and white mottled)

Height:
*4 inches/
10 cm*
**Blooming
Time:**
April–May

Waldsteinia ternata

Siberian Barren Strawberry ✿
Also Known as: Yellow Strawberry

Family: Rose plants *(Rosaceae)*
Native to: Central and Eastern Europe, Siberia, Japan
Bloom: Small, yellow flowers resembling strawberry
Appearance: Ground-covering growth; with time it inter-weaves to form thick mats by means of above-ground runners; wintergreen, shiny, incised leaves
Location: Half- to deep shade; moist to damp soils rich in nutrients; also tolerates summer drought
Planting: Can be planted from spring to fall
Care: Water during periods of extended drought
Arrangement: Appropriate for under and at the edge of wooded areas (e.g., with *Astilbe*, *Omphalodes*, *Lamiastrum*, and *Pulmonaria*)
Species/Varieties: *W. geoides* (8 in./20 cm, yellow flowers, April–May, rough leaves, does not grow runners); visually similar, but for sunny locations: Golden Cinquefoil, *Potentilla aurea* Goldteller (6 in./15 cm, golden yellow); Spring Cinquefoil, *P. neumanniana* (6 in./15 cm, golden yellow)

Height:
47–59 inches/
120–150 cm
**Blooming
Time:**
July

Yucca filamentosa

Adam's Needle
Also Known as: Bear Grass, Weak-leaf Yucca

Family: Agave plants *(Agavaceae)*
Native to: USA
Bloom: Large panicles with whitish bellflowers
Appearance: Exotic appearance with striking growth and long, pointed, wintergreen leaves
Location: Full sun and warm; porous, fairly dry soils containing lime and rich in nutrients
Planting: Can be planted from spring to fall
Care: If long, woody shoots are cut back to around 8 in./20 cm, they grow anew; remove flowers after first blooming; needs protection during winter in cold areas
Arrangement: Use solitary (e.g., with *Anaphalis, Bergenia, Gypsophila, Lavandula, Salvia, Sedum,* and *Stachys*)
Species/Varieties: Polar Bear (59 in./150 cm), Elegantissima (47 in./120 cm, white, erect foliage), Rosenglocke (pink bloom); *Y. × karlsruhensis* (39 in./100 cm, soft pink flowers, July–Aug., narrow leaves, frosted blue); *Y. flaccida* Golden Sword (39 in./100 cm, yellow striped leaves, protect during winter)

173

Annuals and Biennials

from A to Z

Long-lasting bloomers generally show
the bright colors of their flowers without
interruption from May through the fall.
The annuals are especially good for filling
in open spots, for they develop their
flowering beauty within a matter of a few
weeks. In order to prolong the blooming
in a flowerbed, they can be combined
with perennials and bulb plants.

Height:
*4–16 inches/
10–40 cm*
**Blooming
Time:**
May–Oct.

Ageratum houstonianum

Garden Ageratum
Also Known as: Floss Flower

Family: Compositae *(Asteraceae)*
Native to: Mexico, Guatemala, Belize
Bloom: Blue, violet, pink, or white flowers in umbels
Appearance: Annual; bushy, erect growth; notched, oval leaves
grow on branched stems
Location: Sun to partial shade, but not too hot; moist soils
rich in nutrients
Planting: Sow indoors from January to March; plant outdoors
after danger of frost has passed (mid–May)
Care: The low varieties in particular rot if kept too moist.
Arrangement: Harmonizes well with *Cleome,* pink and white
Cosmos, and white, blue, or purple *Verbena*. Attractive color
contrasts with orange *Calendula* and *Tagetes*.
Notes: The tall varieties are good for cutting.
Species/Varieties: Blue Horizon (24 in./60 cm, light blue, →
illus.), Leilani Blue, (medium blue, medium height), Schnitt-
twunder (28 in./70 cm, medium blue), Old Grey (20 in./50
cm, blue-gray)

175

Height:
*59–87 inches/
150–220 cm*
**Blooming
Time:**
July–Sept.

Alcea rosea

Hollyhock
Also Known as: Althea rosea

Family: Mallow plants *(Malvaceae)*
Native to: Southwest Asia
Bloom: Large, single to double bowl-shaped flowers open on the side and arranged on long spikes
Appearance: Biennial; erect, not always sturdy; rough, rounded leaves in matte green; self-seeding
Location: Sunny and warm; porous, relatively moist soils rich in nutrients
Planting: Sow April–June, move outdoors in late summer
Care: Cutting back after the first flowering boosts vitality
Arrangement: Looks attractive against walls and fences; good companions include *Campanula, Cosmos, Delphinium, Leucanthemum, Paeonia,* and *Verbena bonariensis*
Species/Varieties: Many varieties, such as Chater's series: (double flowers); *Alcea* hybrids: Park Allee (yellow, semidouble), Park Rondell (pink, semidouble); *A. ficigolia* (single, various colors); *A. rosea* var. *nigra* (black-red)

Height:
*8–51 inches/
20–130 cm*
**Blooming
Time:**
June–Oct.

Antirrhinum majus

Snapdragon ❀

Family: Figwort plants *(Scrophulariaceae)*
Native to: Iberian Peninsula, France
Bloom: Lush, erect flower clusters in all colors except blue;
often multicolored
Appearance: Annual; generally bushy, erect growth, some-
times protruding; lanceolate, pointed leaves
Location: Sun; loose, fairly moist soils rich in nutrients
Planting: Start indoors as early as February and set out in
mid–May
Care: Continually remove blooms that have gone by; water
during drought
Arrangement: Attractive contrast to *Aster, Calendula, Cosmos,
Leucanthemum, Rudbeckia, Tagetes,* and *Zinnia*
Notes: The tall varieties are good for cut flowers.
Species/Varieties: Many varieties and series, such as Ribbon
series (red, pink, bronze, yellow, and white), Rocket series (28
in./70 cm, in the same colors, good for cutting), Sultan series
(lower, bicolor, in rainbow colors), Lavender variety

Height:
*6–12 inches/
15–30 cm*
**Blooming
Time:**
May–Oct.

Begonia Hybrids

Ice Begonia ✿

Family: Begonia plants *(Begoniaceae)*
Bloom: Small, bowl-shaped flowers in pink, red, or white
Appearance: Annual; bushy, erect growth; shiny, somewhat fleshy, oval leaves in green, sometimes brown-red
Location: Sun to partial shade, warm; porous soils rich in nutrients, moist but not wet or cold; also tolerates quite a bit of drought and even shade
Planting: Can be started indoors as early as December; light germinator; set out in May
Care: Needs a lot of nutrients
Arrangement: Usually used in fairly large groups; goes with such plants as *Antirrhinum, Heliotropium, Nicotiana,* and *Salvia*
Species/Varieties: Numerous varieties, such as Marsala series (blooms scarlet, pink, white, white with red margin, dark foliage), Doublet series (red, pink, or white, double blooms, also suited to shade), tuberous hybrid group (suited to shade, single or double blooms in yellow, orange, red, and white, also bicolor)

Height:
*4–8 inches/
10–20 cm*
**Blooming
Time:**
March–May

Bellis perennis

Common Daisy ✿
Also Known as: English Daisy

Family: Compositae *(Asteraceae)*
Native to: Europe, Turkey, Syria, Palestine
Bloom: Pink, red, or white pompom flowers, sometimes bicolor
Appearance: Biennial; long, rounded leaves in basal rosettes, leafless flower stems
Location: Sun to partial shade; moist to damp, porous soils rich in nutrients; quite winter-hardy, but doesn't like hard frost
Planting: Sow in June or July and set out in the fall
Care: Cover young plants during the winter.
Arrangement: Goes well with other spring bloomers such as *Myosotis, Viola,* and bulb flowers
Notes: Not particularly long-stemmed, but still good for cutting
Species/Varieties: Habanera series (double blooms, sometimes bicolor), Pomponette series (double blooms in white, pink, and red), Roggli series (double blooms), Tasso series in varieties such as Strawberries and Cream, Dunkelrosa, and Hellrosa

Height:
*8–24 inches/
20–60 cm*
**Blooming
Time:**
June–Oct.

Calendula officinalis

Pot Marigold ✿

Family: Compositae *(Asteraceae)*
Native to: Southern Europe
Bloom: Yellow and orange radiate blooms, single to double
Appearance: Annual; bushy, erect growth; oval leaves; self-seeding
Location: Sunny and warm; loose soils rich in nutrients; moist to moderately dry
Planting: Sow indoors as early as February, or sow directly outdoors starting in April
Care: Cut off wilted blooms
Arrangement: The bright color spots contrast with blue and violet blooms such as *Ageratum, Delphinium, Heliotropium,* and *Salvia.* Harmonizes with other yellow flowers such as *Coreopsis, Rudbeckia,* and *Solidago.*
Notes: Cut blooms for the vase as they open up.
Species/Varieties: Calypso (orange and yellow, sturdy stems), Princess (20 in./50 cm, orange and golden yellow, double blooms), Pacific Beauty series (double, also bicolor varieties)

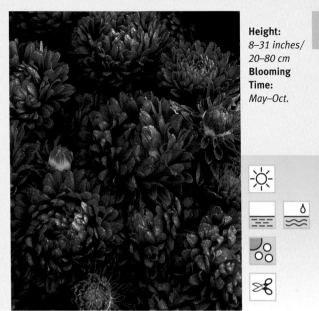

Height:
*8–31 inches/
20–80 cm*
**Blooming
Time:**
May–Oct.

C

Callistephus chinensis

China Aster ✿

Family: Compositae *(Asteraceae)*
Native to: China
Bloom: Single to fully double radiate blooms in nearly all colors, sometimes bicolor and with needle-shaped flower petals
Appearance: Annual; bushy, erect growth; lanceolate to oval toothed leaves
Location: Sunny and warm; moist to damp soils rich in nutrients
Planting: Start indoors as early as February, or sow directly outdoors starting in April
Care: Keep from drying out
Arrangement: Contrasts with blue and violet blooms (e.g., *Ageratum, Delphinium, Heliotripium, Salvia*); harmonizes with yellow flowers such as *Coreopsis, Rudbeckia*, and *Solidago*
Notes: Continually damp soil helps combat aster yellows; also look for resistent varieties
Species/Varieties: Many varieties, such as Stella series (28 in./ 70 cm, single flowers), Matsumoto series (24 in./60 cm, semidouble)

Height:
16–28 inches/
40–70 cm
**Blooming
Time:**
June–Aug.

Campanula medium

Canterbury Bells

Family: Bellflower plants *(Campanulaceae)*
Native to: France, Italy
Bloom: Large bellflowers in erect panicles in dark blue, pink, or white
Appearance: Biennial; the leaf rosettes form in the first year; in the second year, flower stems equipped with oval, notched, and slightly hairy leaves appear
Location: Sunny and warm; porous soils rich in nutrients, but free of standing water
Planting: Sow in June or July and set out starting at the end of August
Care: Water during extended drought; fertilize regularly
Arrangement: Goes well with other multicolored, blooming, country garden flowers such as *Alcea, Calendula, Delphinium, Dianthus barbatus, Malva, Paeonia, Papaver,* and *Phlox*
Notes: The blooms are good for cutting.
Species/Varieties: Alba (white), Calycanthema (double bell-flowers in blue, pink, and white), Rosea (pink), Muse series (22–28 in./55–70 cm, in Pink, Violet, and White)

Height:
*32–47 inches/
80–120 cm*
**Blooming
Time:**
July–Oct.

Cleome spinosa

Spider Flower

Family: Caper plants *(Capparaceae)*
Native to: South America
Bloom: Odd, large bunch of flowers consisting of white, pink, violet, or reddish individual blooms with long stamens
Appearance: Annual; erect, bulky growth; digitate leaves in clusters of five or as many as seven
Location: Sunny and warm; porous, moist to moderately dry soils
Planting: Sow indoors as early as March and set out at the end of May or later, for it needs warm soil
Care: For bushy growth, support young plants
Arrangement: Impressive in summer and mixed flowerbeds; goes well with *Cosmos, Delphinium, Echinacea, Eupatorium,* and *Verbena bonariensis*
Notes: The blooms are good for cutting.
Species/Varieties: Linde Armstrong (mauve blooms, olive-green foliage); *C. hassleriana* (32–39 in./80–100 cm, various colors, July–Sept.)

183

Height:
*24–47 inches/
60–120 cm*
**Blooming
Time:**
June–Oct.

Cosmos bipinnatus

Mexican Aster ✿

Family: Compositae *(Asteraceae)*
Native to: Mexico, Central America
Bloom: Large, single bowl-shaped flowers in pink, red, or white, usually with a yellow center; sometimes bicolor
Appearance: Annual; erect, bushy growth, vigorous; showy, light green, double feathery leaves
Location: Sunny and warm; porous soils rich in nutrients, also moist soils
Planting: Start seeds as early as the end of March, set out plants starting in May
Care: Stake taller varieties if necessary
Arrangement: Attractive specimen plant, for example, with *Achillea, Delphinium, Monarda, Phlox,* and *Verbena bonariensis*
Notes: Cut blooms for the vase as they open up
Species/Varieties: Picotee (white with red margin), Sonata series (compact growth): Pink Blush (pink, red margin), Carmine (carmine); Chocolate Cosmos, *C. atrosanguineus* (20 in./50 cm, burgundy red); Sulphur Cosmos, *C. sulphureus* (16–24 in./40–60 cm, orange or yellow flowers)

184

Height:
16–24 inches/
40–60 cm
Blooming
Time:
May–Aug.

Dianthus barbatus

Sweet William

Family: Pink or Carnation family *(Caryophyllaceae)*
Native to: Europe (mainland)
Bloom: Small individual flowers in umbrella-like umbels, in shades of red and pink, white, and bicolor; petals are slightly fringed on the margin
Appearance: Biennial; in the first year, only the leaf rosettes form, with lanceolate, dark green leaves; in the second year, the plant grows erect
Location: Sun; porous soils rich in nutrients
Planting: Sow from May to July; plant in their final location in the fall
Care: Cover in the winter
Arrangement: Goes well with other country garden plants such as *Campanula, Delphinium, Leucanthemum,* and *Tanacetum*
Notes: Durable cut flowers
Species/Varieties: Many varieties such as Atrosanguineus (dark purple-red), Bodestolz Mix (20 in./50 cm), Bouquet Purple (20 in./50 cm, luminescent violet), Pink Beauty (pink)

Height:
*8–35 inches/
20–90 cm*
**Blooming
Time:**
April–July

Erysimum Hybrids

Bowles Mauve

Family: Mustard or Cabbage plants *(Brassicaceae)*
Bloom: Small flowers in tight, erect clusters, in yellow, red, orange, purple, and pink; often bicolor
Appearance: Biennial; bushy, fairly sturdy, erect growth; lanceolate leaves; widely varying height
Location: Sunny and warm; porous and rather nutrient-poor soils; likes lime
Planting: Sow outdoors in the summer.
Care: Cover in the winter; susceptible to damage from snails and slugs
Arrangement: Goes well with *Calendula, Erigeron karvinskianus, Papaver nudicaule, Santolina, Sedum,* and *Viola cornuta*
Notes: The flowers have a sweet fragrance.
Species/Varieties: Bowles Mauve (35 in./90 cm, violet flowers that last especially long, blue-green foliage, → illus.), Orange Flame (8 in./20 cm, luminous orange flowers), Yellow Bird (12 in./30 cm, golden yellow); Orange Cheiri or Aegean Wallflower, *E. cheiri* (12–28 in./30–70 cm, March–May, varieties in yellow, orange, and red)

Height:
*16–98 inches/
40–250 cm*
**Blooming
Time:**
July–Oct.

Helianthus annuus

Sunflower ✿

Family: Compositae *(Asteraceae)*
Native to: USA, Northern Mexico
Bloom: Large to very large radiate flowers in yellow, red, or brownish red; single (with dark or yellow center) to double
Appearance: Annual; erect or bushy growth; tall varieties generally single-stemmed; lower varieties also branched; not always sturdy; rough, pointed, oval leaves
Location: Sunny and warm; loose, moderately dry to moist soils rich in nutrients
Planting: Best sown right in the flowerbed in April; otherwise, start in pots and set out starting mid-May
Care: Fertilize regularly.
Arrangement: Larger varieties are used individually, shorter ones in groups, for example with *Delphinium* and *Tithonia*
Notes: There are pollen-free varieties.
Species/Varieties: Countless varieties such as Prado series (51 in./130 cm, yellow or red-brown, multiple blooms), Sunrich series (67 in./170 cm): Gold, Lemon, Orange, and Teddybear (16 in./40 cm, yellow, double)

Height:
*20–39 inches/
50–100 cm*
**Blooming
Time:**
July–Sept.

Helichrysum bracteatum

Strawflower Daisy
Also Known as: Paper Daisy, Everlasting Daisy

Family: Compositae *(Asteraceae)*
Native to: Australia
Bloom: Red, pink, orange, yellow, or white radiate blooms
that feel like dry straw
Appearance: Annual or biennial; erect, bushy, branched
growth; lanceolate leaves
Location: Sunny and warm; normal, porous soils moderately
rich in nutrients
Planting: Sow directly into the flowerbed at the end of April,
or start indoors in March or April and set out in mid-May
Care: Avoid fertilizing excessively
Arrangement: Goes well with gray foliage such as *Anaphalis* or
with *Calendula, Heliotropium,* and other dry flowers
Notes: Cut blooms for the vase shortly before they open up;
for drying, hang flowers upside down.
Species/Varieties: Monstrosum (32 in./80 cm, several colors),
Sundaze series (blooms in various colors)

Height:
12–20 inches/
30–50 cm
Blooming
Time:
May–Sept.

Heliotropium arborescens

Heliotrope

Family: Borage plants *(Boraginaceae)*
Native to: Peru
Bloom: Small, individual, violet flowers in luxurious umbels
Appearance: Raised as an annual in a moderate latitude;
bushy, branched, loose growth; dark green, furrowed leaves
Location: Sun to partial shade and warm; porous, moist soils
rich in nutrients, but not in wet locations; even the blooms
suffer from dampness (rain)
Planting: Seldom sown, but if it is, indoors from January to
March; set out young plants in mid-May
Care: Cut off blooms that have gone by
Arrangement: The violet flowers go well with shades of
orange and yellow (e.g., *Calendula, Coreopsis, Helenium,
Helichrysum, Rudbeckia, Solidago,* and *Tagetes*)
Notes: Poisonous! The flowers have a strong fragrance of
vanilla.
Species/Varieties: Marine (24 in./60 cm, → illus.) and Mini
Marine (12 in./30 cm)

Height:
*12–35 inches/
30–90 cm*
**Blooming
Time:**
June–Sept.

Matthiola incana

Garden Stock
Also Known as: Common Stock

Family: Mustard or Cabbage plants *(Brassicaceae)*
Native to: Balkans, Southern Europe, British Isles, Cyprus
Bloom: Clusters of inflorescences with individual white, pink, red, purple, or yellow flowers; single and double blooms
Appearance: Grown as annual or biennial; sturdy, erect growth, usually slightly branched shoot; lanceolate leaf
Location: Sunny and warm; moist, porous soils rich in nutrients and containing lime; no standing water or drought
Planting: Sow indoors starting in February or March and set out in May; plants that bloom double display light green leaves; single blooms have dark green foliage
Care: Continually cut off blooms that have gone by
Arrangement: Goes well with other country garden plants such as *Campanula, Delphinium, Leucanthemum,* and *Tanacetum*
Notes: Cut for the vase when two-thirds of the clusters have bloomed
Species/Varieties: Miracle Formula Mix (32 in./80 cm), among others

Height:
6–16 inches/
15–40 cm
**Blooming
Time:**
April–June

M

Myosotis sylvatica

Forget-Me-Not ✿

Family: Borage plants *(Boraginaceae)*
Native to: Europe, Northwestern Africa
Bloom: Small, blue, pink, or white bunches of blooms
Appearance: Grown as a biennial; loose, bushy growth with rough, lanceolate leaves; self-seeding
Location: Sun; moist to damp, porous soils rich in nutrients
Planting: Sow in late summer; set out in the fall, or set out in the spring after wintering over in frost-free conditions
Care: Cover young plants for the winter; never let the soil dry out
Arrangement: Attractive with other spring bloomers such as *Bellis, Fritillaria, Iris, Hyacinthoides,* and *Viola*
Notes: The blooms are good for cutting.
Species/Varieties: Amethyst (dark blue), Blue Ball (gleaming blue), Compindi (dark blue), Indigo Compacta (gleaming blue), Rosylva (pink), Victoria Pink (pink), Victoria White (white)

Height:
*12–28 inches/
30–70 cm*
**Blooming
Time:**
June–Oct.

Nicotiana × sanderae

Flowering Tobacco

Family: Nightshade plants *(Solanaceae)*
Bloom: Individual tubular, white, light yellow, pink, or red flowers that open into a star shape and are arranged in multiple loose clusters
Appearance: Annual; basal leaf rosette from which the branched inflorescence arises; oval leaves
Location: Sunny and warm; moist, porous soils rich in nutrients
Planting: Start seeds in February or March; set plants out starting in May
Care: Water during fairly extended drought
Arrangement: Use in small groups, for example with *Callistephus, Cosmos,* and *Delphinium*
Notes: Susceptible to snails and slugs; the plant is poisonous, although to a lesser extent than *N. sylvestris* and *N. tabacum*
Species/Varieties: Many varieties, such as Fragrant Delight (47 in./120 cm, fragrant at night, multicolored mixture), Lime Green (39 in./100 cm, yellow-green); *N. alata* (12–24 in./30–60 cm, strongly scented blooms); White Shooting Stars, *N. sylvestris*

Height:
*12–35 inches/
30–90 cm*
**Blooming
Time:**
July–Oct.

R

Rudbeckia hirta

Black-eyed Susan ✿

Family: Compositae *(Asteraceae)*
Native to: USA
Bloom: Yellow, orange, or brown-red tongued flowers surrounding a dark brown or yellow-green, rounded center; often bicolor, single to fully double
Appearance: Annual or biennial; however, in mild locations, it can live even longer; sturdy, erect, clustered growth; dark green, rough, oval leaves
Location: Sunny and warm; normal to damp soils rich in nutrients
Planting: Easiest to sow directly in the flowerbed in May
Care: Cut off flowers that have gone by; continuous cutting for the vase stimulates the plant to form new blooms
Arrangement: Goes well with *Antirrhinum, Aster, Delphinium, Helenium, Heliotropium, Phlox, Salvia, Vernonia,* and *Verbena*
Species/Varieties: Many varieties such as Goldilocks (golden yellow, semidouble), Prairie Sun (golden and cream-yellow, single); Toto series (12 in./30 cm, yellow and bronze-yellow)

Height:
*20–24 inches/
50–60 cm*
**Blooming
Time:**
June–Sept.

Salvia coccinea

Scarlet Sage

Family: Mint plants *(Lamiaceae)*
Native to: USA, Mexico, Caribbean
Bloom: Scarlet, pink, or white; also bicolor lipped flowers in loose, heady panicles
Appearance: Annual to biennial; erect, bushy growth; dark green, oval leaves
Location: Sunny and warm; moist, porous soils rich in nutients
Planting: Start in March and set outdoors starting in May
Care: Water and fertilize regularly
Arrangement: The bright red type goes best with blue or white (e.g, *Delphinium, Heliotropum,* and *Leucanthemum*)
Species/Varieties: Lady in Red (→ illus.), Red Indian (red), Snow Nymph (white and red), Coral Nymph (pink-white); *S. involucrate* (31–39 in./80–100 cm, pink, July–Sept.); Scarlet or Tropical Sage, *S. splendens* (8–20 in./20–50 cm, May–Oct.), Fire on Ice (red, apricot-colored bract), Fire Star (scarlet), Pharao Burgundy (burgundy-red, light stripes)

Height:
20–31 inches/
50–80 cm
Blooming Time:
May–Oct.

Salvia farinacea

Mealy-cup Sage

Family: Mint plants *(Lamiaceae)*
Native to: New Mexico, Texas
Bloom: Small, dark blue or white lipped flowers in narrow heads
Appearance: Usually biennial; clustered, erect, branched growth; the stems are powdered with white
Location: Sun to partial shade; moist, porous soils rich in nutrients
Planting: Sow in a warm location in March or April and set out in the flowerbed starting in mid–May
Care: Can overwinter in cool conditions
Arrangement: Goes well with other summer flowers and perennials such as *Calendula, Helenium, Heliopsos, Rudbeckia,* and *Tithonia*
Species/Varieties: Victoria (dark blue, → illus.), Silver (silver-white), Innocence (silver-white); Cambridge Blue, *S. patens* (20–31 in./50–80 cm, gentian blue, June–Sept.); *S. uliginosa* (55 in./140 cm, gleaming blue flowers on arched panicles, Aug.–Sept., plant only in the spring, needs protection during the winter)

Height:
*31–39 inches/
80–100 cm*
**Blooming
Time:**
July–Aug.

Salvia sclarea
Clary Sage

Family: Mint family *(Lamiaceae)*
Native to: Southern and Eastern Europe, Caucasus, Southwest Asia, Northwestern Africa, Central Asia
Bloom: Individual pink, violet, or white flowers in large panicles, pink spathes
Appearance: Biennial; the basal leaf rosettes form in the first year, and the branched inflorescences in the second; large leaves, tinged with gray; self-seeding
Location: Sun; porous and fairly lean soils
Planting: Sow in the summer and set out in the fall
Care: Avoid fertilizing excessively
Arrangement: Particularly attractive with pink flowers such as *Cleome and Cosmos bipinnatus* and with blue *Salvia*
Notes: Fragrant plant
Species/Varieties: Piemont (dark red-purple), Vatican White (32 in./80 cm, white flowers, white spathe); Painted Sage, *S. viridis* (16–24 in./40–60 cm, inconspicuous flowers, impressive violet, pink, red, or cream-white spathe, June–Sept.)

Height:
*8–16 inches/
20–40 cm*
**Blooming
Time:**
May–Oct.

Tagetes patula

Marigold ✿

Family: Compositae *(Asteraceae)*
Native to: Mexico, Guatemala
Bloom: Single, semi- to fully double blooms in yellow, orange, or red-brown; also bicolor
Appearance: Annual; erect, bushy growth; very feathery leaves
Location: Sun; normal garden soils, damp to moderately dry; not too nutrient-rich
Planting: Start in March and plant in May (earlier blooming)
Care: Water during extended drought
Arrangement: Shorter varieties as border, otherwise gleaming, colorful areas among *Heliotropium* or blue *Salvia*; also attractive with other yellow blooms such as *Calendula* and *Solidago*
Notes: Serious threat from snails and slugs; taller varieties good for cutting; older varieties have a tangy, strong fragrance
Species/Varieties: Many varieties; American Marigold, *T. erecta* (12–47 in./30–120 cm, large blooms); Starfire, *T. Tenuifolia* (8–12 in./20–30 cm, single blooms, showy)

Height:
*8–28 inches/
20–70 cm*
**Blooming
Time:**
June–Oct.

Tanacetum parthenium

Feverfew

Family: Compositae *(Asteraceae)*
Native to: Balkans, Turkey
Bloom: Small, white or yellow daisy flowers, also double, in upright umbels
Appearance: Usually annual; bushy, branched growth with incised leaflets; stems not always sturdy
Location: Sun; moist to damp, porous soils rich in nutrients
Planting: Sow starting in February; keep cuttings over the winter
Care: Water during extended drought
Arrangement: Goes with most summer flowers and perennials
Notes: Blooms keep well in the vase; plant is mildly poisonous.
Species/Varieties: Golden Moss (12 in./30 cm, yellow, double), Roya (20 in./50 cm, single bloom, white with yellow center), Snowball (12 in./30 cm, white, double), Tetra White (large, double flowers), White Pompom (double); Corymbflower Tansy, *T. corymbosum* (32 in./80 cm, white flower umbels, May–June, lives for several years)

Height:
31–71 inches/
80–180 cm
Blooming Time:
July–Oct.

Tithonia rotundifolia

Mexican Sunflower

Family: Compositae *(Asteraceae)*
Native to: Mexico
Bloom: Bright orange or yellow radiate blooms with yellow-orange or golden yellow center
Appearance: Annual; bushy, sturdy, erect growth
Location: Sun; moist, porous soils that never dry out and are rich in nutrients
Planting: Sow indoors in March or April and plant outdoors starting in mid-May; better to sow directly in May
Care: Water during extended drought; young plants can be pruned to stimulate greater branching
Arrangement: Impressive color; appropriate for beds in sunny colors (e.g., *Calendula, Helenium,* and *Rudbeckia*) or as contrast to blue and violet flowers (e.g., *Delphinium, Heliotropium, Salvia,* and *Verbena bonariensis*)
Notes: Cut blooms as they are opening.
Species/Varieties: Fackel (up to 59 in./150 cm, orange), Fiesta del Sol (16 in./40 cm, light orange), Yellow (47 in./120 cm, yellow)

Height:
*12–157 inches/
30–400 cm*
**Blooming
Time:**
July–Oct.

Tropaeolum majus

Nasturtium

Family: Nasturtium plants *(Tropaeolaceae)*
Native to: Colombia, Ecuador, Peru
Bloom: Large, funnel-shaped blooms in orange, red, pink, or yellow; sometimes semi- or fully double
Appearance: Annual; climbing or creeping shoots; large, rounded leaves; top of leaves is darker than the bottom.
Location: Sun to partial shade and warm; porous, humusy, fairly damp soils; not too rich in nutrients
Planting: Sow directly outdoors starting at the end of April
Care: Avoid fertilizing too much
Arrangement: Attractive on climbing trellises and as ground cover (e.g., with *Calendula, Cosmos sulphureus, Helenium, Heliopsis, Rudbeckia,* and *Verbena bonariensis*).
Notes: The blooms and buds are edible.
Species/Varieties: Many varieties such as Empress of India (12 in./30 cm, red, dark foliage), Peach Melba (12 in./30 cm, cream-yellow with red); Canary Creeper, *T. peregrinum* (200–300 cm, small, yellow, fringed blooms, May–Oct., showy foliage)

Height:
*39–47 inches/
100–120 cm*
**Blooming
Time:**
June–Oct.

Verbena bonariensis

Purpletop Verbena

Family: Verbena plants *(Verbenaceae)*
Native to: Brazil, Argentina
Bloom: Small, violet blooms arranged in umbels
Appearance: Usually annual; bulky, erect growth; dark green, narrow leaves
Location: Sunny and warm; normal garden soils rich in nutrients; does not like heavy soils
Planting: Start indoors from January to March; the seeds sprout better if they are kept cool (40°F/5°C) for a week
Care: No particular requirements
Arrangement: Attractive, filigree effect among other summer flowers and perennials such as *Aster, Cleome, Cosmos, Helenium, Lavatera, Rudbeckia, Solidago,* and *Tithonia*
Notes: The blooms are good for cutting.
Species/Varieties: Coarse Verbena, *V. rigida* (8–16 in./20–40 cm, blue-violet, June–Oct.) Blue Vervain, *V. hastata* (47 in./120 cm, violet candelabra-like inflorescences, July–Sept.)
V. stricta (24 in./60 cm, purple, gray-green foliage)

Height:
*4–10 inches/
10–25 cm*
**Blooming
Time:**
*March–May,
Oct.–Nov.*

Viola × wittrockiana

Pansy

Family: Violet plants *(Violaceae)*
Bloom: Large blooms in all colors, also multicolored; flower petals sometimes undulating or significantly pleated
Appearance: Biennial; low, bushy, erect growth; notched, oval leaves
Location: Sun to light shade; moist to damp, porous soils rich in nutrients
Planting: Set out in the fall or spring
Care: If plants are set out in the fall, cover for the winter.
Arrangement: Plant in groups; goes well with other spring bloomers such as *Bellis, Heuchera, Hyacinthus, Myositis, Narcussus, Tulipa,* bulb flowers, and grasses.
Species/Varieties: Countless varieties and series, such as Bingo, Cello, Delta Premium, Dynamite, Experimental, Fancy, Karma; all series come in various pure color shades and a dark eye such as Cello Red with Blotch, Fancy with Blotch, Delta Blue with Blotch, Delta Premium Pure Yellow, Delta Premium Yellow with Purple Wing

Height:
*12–39 inches/
30–100 cm*
**Blooming
Time:**
July–Sept.

Zinnia elegans

Zinnia ✿

Family: Compositae *(Asteraceae)*
Native to: Mexico
Bloom: Single, semi- to fully double blooms in yellow, orange, red, pink, white, plus multicolored; smaller and larger varieties
Appearance: Annual; erect, clustered growth, more or less branched; oval, pointed leaves
Location: Sunny and warm, moist to damp soils rich in nutrients
Planting: Start indoors as early as April, set out starting in May, or sow directly outdoors
Care: Water during drought; cut off blooms that have gone by
Arrangement: In small groups, for example with *Antirrhinum, Callistephus, Cosmos, Delphinium,* and *Leucanthemum*
Notes: Cut flowers keep well.
Species/Varieties: Numerous varieties such as Envy Double (yellow-green, double); *Z. angustifolia* (16–20 in./40–50 cm, white, yellow, orange, single, low-lying shoots); *A. haageana* (12–16 in./30–40 cm, white, yellow, orange, brown-red, single or double)

Bulb and Tuber Plants

from A to Z

The first colors in the spring are from bulb and tuber plants. They are also colorful eyecatchers in the flowerbed during the summer and fall. Many types also provide attractive cutting flowers. Most are winter-hardy; a few of the underground storage organs require protection from frost during the winter.

Height:
24–39 inches/
60–100 cm
**Blooming
Time:**
June–Aug.

A

Allium aflatunense

Persian Onion

Family: Leek plants *(Alliaceae)*
Native to: Central Asia
Bloom: Small, single flowers that are arranged together in the shape of a ball; colors include shades of red, pink, and purple
Appearance: Winter-hardy bulb plant; the leaves are narrow and similar to grass, and grow after flowering
Location: Sunny and warm; porous soils
Planting: The best time to plant is October.
Care: Let wilted balls stand over winter.
Arrangement: Place randomly in small clusters or several plants individually in the bed, for example with *Artemisia, Centranthus, Crambe, Gypsophila, Iris barbata, Nepeta, Phlomis, Sedum,* and *Stachys*
Species/Varieties: Purple Sensation (24–31 in./60–80 cm, purple violet); Ornamental Onion, *A. christophii* (16 in./ 40 cm, large, pink-purple balls of flowers, June–July, blue-green foliage); Roundheaded Leek, *A. sphaerocephalon* (28 in./70 cm, fairly small, oval inflorescences in dark purple, July–Aug.)

Height:
*6–8 inches/
15–20 cm*
**Blooming
Time:**
March–April

Anemone blanda

Grecian Windflower
Also Known as: Greek Thimbleweed

Family: Buttercup or Crowfoot plants *(Ranunculaceae)*
Native to: Balkans, Turkey, Caucasus
Bloom: Single, blue, pink, red, or white radiate flowers
Appearance: Winter-hardy rhizomes; soft, sometimes incised foliage; loose growth; self-sowing in appropriate locations
Location: Partial to full shade; moist to moderately damp soils rich in nutrients; likes lime
Planting: Plant in fall or spring
Care: Cover with leaves for the winter in cold areas
Arrangement: Attractive under leaf trees with *Astilbe, Bergenia, Brunnera, Corydalis, Omphalodes, Polygonatum,* tulips, and grasses such as *Carex sylvatica, Luzula,* and *Millium effusum*
Notes: The plant is mildly poisonous.
Species/Varieties: Blue Shades (blue, → illus.), Charmer (dark pink), Radar (white with red margin), White Splendor (white); Wood Anemone, *A. nemorosa* (6–8 in./15–20 cm, white, indigenous), Alba Plena (white, double), Dee Day (light blue), Robinsoniana (light blue), Seemannii (soft yellow)

Height:
*4–6 inches/
10–15 cm*
**Blooming
Time:**
March–April

C

Chionodoxa luciliae

Glory of the Snow ✿

Family: Hyacinth plants *(Hyacinthaceae)*
Native to: Turkey
Bloom: Star-shaped blooms, purple-blue or pink with white eye, or pure white
Appearance: Winter-hardy bulb flower with narrow, linear leaves that retract after blooming; erect flower stems
Location: Sun to partial shade; normal, porous soils rich in nutrients
Planting: In the fall, insert bulbs to a depth of 2–4 in./5–10 cm.
Care: Remove leaves when they turn yellow.
Arrangement: Set out in several small groups; readily goes wild, even in the lawn; goes well with *Bellis, Crocus, Glaanthus, Iberis, Myosotis,* and *Viola cornuta*
Species/Varieties: Alba (white), Pink Giant (pink, prolific bloomer); Gigantea group (like the variety, but higher, larger blooms); *C. forbesii,* and Lesser Glory of the Snow, *C. sardensis* (lower, showier blooms)

Height:
6–10 inches/
15–25 cm
Blooming Time:
May–June

Convallaria majalis

Lily of the Valley

Family: Lily of the Valley plants *(Convallariaceae)*
Native to: Europe to Western Asia
Bloom: Small, white, nodding bellflowers in panicles; red fruits subsequently develop from the flowers
Appearance: Winter-hardy plant that propagates through rhizomes; broad, oval to lanceolate, leathery leaves
Location: Partial to full shade; moderately dry to moist, porous soils; with enough moisture, also thrives in a sunny location
Planting: Can be planted from spring to fall
Care: Divide with a spade if it spreads too much
Arrangement: Tends to go wild under leaf trees; plant in several small groups, for example with *Epimedium, Heuchera, Hosta, Omphalodes, Pulmonaria, Tiarella, Waldsteinia,* and shade grasses
Notes: All plant parts are poisonous. The flowers are good for cutting and have a strong fragrance.
Species/Varieties: Grandiflora (large flowers), Rosea (soft pink)

Height:
*6–10 inches/
15–25 cm*
**Blooming
Time:**
April–May

C

Corydalis cava

Bird-in-a-Bush

Family: Fumitory family *(Fumariaceae)*
Native to: Europe (mainland), Turkey, Caucasus, Northern Iran
Bloom: Small, spurred blooms in clusters, purple, pink, or white
Appearance: Winter-hardy tuber plant; bushy, erect growth with showy, multiply feathered, blue-green foliage that recedes after blooming
Location: Preferably partial shade; moist to damp, humusy and porous soils; likes to be under leaf trees; self-seeding in appropriate locations
Planting: Plant 2–4 in./5–10 cm deep in the fall
Care: It's best to leave it alone and let it grow.
Arrangement: In small groups or over broader areas, together with *Chionodoxa, Concallaria, Hosta, Lamium,* and wild crocus
Notes: The plant is poisonous.
Species/Varieties: Blue Panda, *C. flexuosa* (12 in./30 cm, blue); Fumewort, *C. solida* (8 in./20 cm, red, pink, or white, March–April); Rock Fumewort, *Pseudofumaria lutea* (8–12 in./20–30 cm, yellow, May–Sept., self-seeding)

Height:
*24–39 inches/
60–100 cm*
**Blooming
Time:**
July–Sept.

Crocosmia × crocosmiiflora

Crocosmia
Also Known as: Montbretia

Family: Iris plants *(Iridaceae)*
Bloom: Orange, red, or yellow funnel-shaped flowers arranged in heads; slightly overhanging flowers
Appearance: Multiple-year, unreliably winter-hardy bulb plant; long, narrow leaves; growth through runners
Location: Sunny and warm; porous, damp to moderately dry soils rich in nutrients
Planting: Plant in the spring
Care: In the winter, cover with brush and protect from dampness, or dig up the bulbs and keep them dry and frost-free for the winter; cut back in the spring
Arrangement: With its size and later blooming time, it goes well with other summer bloomers such as *Aster, Dahlia, Kniphofia,* and *Salvia*
Notes: The blooms last for a long time in the vase.
Species/Varieties: Lucifer (red, → illus.), Fire King (red), Red King (red, orange center), Bressingham Blaze (orange-red), Firebird (orange), Golden Fleece (yellow), Venus (orange)

Height:
*2–6 inches/
5–15 cm*
**Blooming
Time:**
March–April

Crocus Hybrids

Crocus ✿

Family: Iris plants *(Iridaceae)*
Bloom: Large flower calyx in white, yellow, blue, and violet; often also multicolored or striped
Appearance: Winter-hardy tuber plant; propagates widely over time; narrow, grass-like bunches of leaves, often with white stripes; the foliage recedes after flowering
Location: Sun to partial shade and warm; porous, moist soils; likes it dry in the summer
Planting: Plant 2–4 in./5–10 cm deep in the fall
Care: Remove leaves when they turn yellow
Arrangement: In fairly large groups in the bed or in the sunny edge of wooded areas; attractive with other *Crocus* varieties and *Eranthis*
Notes: Mice like to eat the tubers.
Species/Varieties: Countless varieties and smaller-bloomed wild types: *C. chrysanthus* (yellow or white); Yellow Crocus, *C. flavus* (orange-yellow); *C. tommasinianus* (soft purple); Autumn Crocus, *C. speciosus* (shades of blue and purple, plant in July/Aug., blooms Sept.–Nov.)

Height:
*2–4 inches/
5–10 cm*
**Blooming
Time:**
March–April

Cyclamen coum

Cyclamen

Family: Primrose plants *(Primulacae)*
Native to: Turkey, Caucasus
Bloom: Small, white, pink, or red cyclamen flowers
Appearance: Winter-hardy tuber plant with round, kidney-to heart-shaped leaves; over time, it forms a thick carpet
Location: Likes bright sunlight in the spring, but shade in the summer; porous, humusy, moist soils; likes lime
Planting: Plant about 2 in./5 cm deep in the fall
Care: In cold areas, cover for the winter
Arrangement: Plant in fairly large groups under leaf trees, for example with *Helleborus, Omphalodes,* and *Primula*
Notes: The blooms have only a mild fragrance.
Species/Varieties: Album (white with dark center), Rosa Selektion (soft pink); Hardy Cyclamen, *C. hederifolium* (blooms Sept.–Oct. in red, pink, or white, fragrant, winter protection is advisable, the tubers get larger year by year); *C. purpurascens* (blooms July–Sept./Oct., in pink or red, fragrant and winter-hardy)

Height:
*8–55 inches/
20–150 cm*
**Blooming
Time:**
July–Oct.

D

Dahlia Hybrids
Dahlia

Family: Compositae *(Asteraceae)*
Bloom: Single or semi- to fully double blooms in cactus, semicactus, pompom, ball, anemone, water lily, ruffle, peony, or orchid shape; in all colors except blue, plus bicolor
Appearance: Frost-sensitive tuber plant; bushy, erect growth, not always sturdy; dark green, sometimes reddish, ovate leaves
Location: Sunny and warm; porous, moist soils rich in nutrients
Planting: Set out in mid-May; in October, remove the tubers from the ground and keep them frost-free over the winter
Care: Stake if necessary; remove wilted parts
Arrangement: In mixed beds, good with *Cosmos, Leucanthemella, Lythrum, Physostegia, Pseudolysimachion, Salvia, Tanacetum parthemium, Verbena bonariensis,* and grasses
Notes: Cut flowers keep well; danger of damage from snails and slugs
Species/Varieties: Countless varieties on the market

Height:
2–4 inches/
5–10 cm
**Blooming
Time:**
Feb.–March

Eranthis hyemalis

Winter Aconite ❋

Family: Buttercup or Crowfoot plants *(Ranunculaceae)*
Native to: Southern Europe
Bloom: Single, yellow bowl-shaped flower
Appearance: Winter-hardy tuber plant; deeply incised leaves
that recede after blooming; propagates amply by means of
self-sowing and new tubers
Location: Half-shady to shady; moist to moderately dry,
porous, humusy soils; in spring, likes light and warmth
Planting: Plant about 2 in./5 cm deep in the fall; the tubers
should be put into the ground right away, for they dry out
quickly
Care: Best to let it grow in peace
Arrangement: Likes to go wild under low growth, such as a
the edge of leafy bushes; goes well with *Chionodoxa, Crocus,
Galanthus, Omphalodes,* and *Scilla*
Notes: The blooms emit a strong fragrance.
Species/Varieties: *E. × tubergenii* (sterile cross with larger
flowers), Glory, Guinea Gold (bronze-hued foliage)

Height:
*47–79 inches/
120–200 cm*
**Blooming
Time:**
June–July

E

Eremurus Hybrids

Desert Candle
Also Known as: Foxtail Lily

Family: Asphodel plants *(Asphodelaceae)*
Bloom: Small blooms in long spikes; white, yellow, and orange
Appearance: Winter-hardy; fleshy roots; sturdy, erect flower
stems; narrow, blue-green leaves that turn yellow at blooming
time and then recede
Location: Sunny and warm; on very porous soils preferably
rich in nutrients; likes moisture during the growth phase, but
dry conditions after blooming and during the winter
Planting: Plant 6–8 in./15–20 cm deep in a small hill of sand
in the summer or fall
Care: Protect from dampness during rest period; remove
wilted parts
Arrangement: Looks nice with *Achillea, Anthemis, Asphodeline, Euphorbia, Nepeta, Papaver,* and grasses
Notes: The blooms can be cut for the vase as soon as the first
buds open.
Species/Varieties: *E. robustus* (white); *E. stenophyllus* (yellow)

Height:
*8–12 inches/
20–30 cm*
**Blooming
Time:**
April–May

Fritillaria meleagris

Snake's Head
**Also Known as: Snake's Head, Fritillary, Leper Lily,
Guinea-Hen Flower**

Family: Lily plants *(Liliaceae)*
Native to: Europe (except for the Iberian Peninsula)
Bloom: Nodding bellflower in violet to pink with lighter spots
in checkered pattern or in white
Appearance: Winter-hardy bulb plant with narrow, gray-
green, grass-like foliage that recedes after blooming
Location: Sun to partial shade and warm; damp but porous soils
Planting: Plant 3–4 in./8–10 cm deep in the fall
Care: Water during severe drought
Arrangement: Plant in small groups, for example with
Alchemilla, Euphorbia, Myosotis, and *Tiarella*
Notes: The blooms are good for cutting.
Species/Varieties: Aphrodite (pure white), Emperor (violet),
Jupiter (purple), Poseidon (pink), Saturnus (red); Crown
Imperial, *F. imperialis* is totally different (20–39 in./50–100
cm, blooms in whorls handing beneath a leaf cluster, in
yellow, red, or orange)

Height:
*4–6 inches/
10–15 cm*
**Blooming
Time:**
Feb.–April

G

Galanthus nivalis

Snowdrop ✿

Family: Amaryllis plants *(Amaryllidaceae)*
Native to: Europe (mainland)
Bloom: Small, nodding, bell-shaped flowers, white, with green spots inside; also double blooming
Appearance: Winter-hardy bulb plant with narrow, linear leaves that recede after flowering
Location: Partial shade and cool; moist to damp, clayey soils rich in nutrients; drier after blooming
Planting: Plant 2–3 in./5–8 cm deep in early fall
Care: Remove leaves when they turn yellow
Arrangement: Likes to go wild, preferably under summer-green deciduous trees, for example with *Anemone blanda, Anemone nemorosa, Helleborus, Myosotis,* and wild crocuses
Notes: Fragrant blooms; all parts of the plant are poisonous
Species/Varieties: Flore Pleno (= Plenus, with double blooms), S. Arnot (white), Viridi apice (larger, white-green flowers); *G. elwesii* (6–10 in./15–25 cm, larger, white flowers, fragrant, broader leaves, likes the sun)

Height:
*20–59 inches/
50–150 cm*
**Blooming
Time:**
June–Sept.

Gladiolus Hybrids

Gladiolus

Family: Iris plants *(Iridaceae)*
Bloom: Large, funnel-shaped flowers on long panicles, in all colors except blue; also bicolor and multicolored
Appearance: Frost-sensitive tuber plant; flower stems not always sturdy; ensiform, sturdy, erect leaves
Location: Sunny, warm, and protected; porous, moist to damp soils rich in nutrients
Planting: Plant 4 in./10 cm deep in mid-May; remove from the bed in October and keep frost-free over the winter
Care: Stake if necessary
Arrangement: Plant in small groups, for example with *Cosmos, Echinacea, Helenium, Leucanthemum, Salvia,* and *Tithonia*
Notes: Some flowers are fragrant; all keep for a very long time in a vase; cut them when the panicle begins to bloom
Species/Varieties: Many varieties and groups: Large-flowered Gladiolus (39–59 in./100–150 cm); Baby Gladiolus (20–24 in./50–60 cm); Butterfly Gladiolus (32–39 in./80–100 cm, wavy flower petals); Sword Lily or hardy Gladiolus, *G. communis* (24–39 in./60–100 cm, magenta, light spots, June)

Height:
8–16 inches/
20–40 cm
Blooming Time:
April–May

Hyacinthoides non-scripta

Bluebell ✿

Family: Hyacinth plants *(Hyacinthaceae)*
Native to: British Isles, France, Iberian Peninsula
Bloom: Small, pendent, blue, violet, pink, or white bellflowers in clusters on erect stems
Appearance: Winter-hardy bulb plant; clustered growth, broad, linear leaves; prone to spreading through self-seeding
Location: Sun to partial shade and warm; moist to damp, porous soils rich in nutrients
Planting: Plant 4–6 in./10–15 cm deep in the fall; don't leave the bulbs uncovered very long, for they dry out quickly
Care: Remove flowers that have gone by to prevent self-seeding.
Arrangement: Attractive in borders with wooded areas or in mixed beds, for example with *Brunnera, Epimedium, Helleborus,* and *Hosta*
Notes: Blooms can be cut for the vase.
Species/Varieties: Spanish Bluebell, *H. hispanica* (taller growth), Blue Bird (deep blue), Dainty Maid (pink), Excelsior (violet), La Grandesse (white), Miss World (seedlings), Rosabella (pink), White City (white)

Height:
8–12 inches/
20–30 cm
Blooming
Time:
April–May

Hyacinthus orientalis

Common Hyacinth

Family: Hyacinth plants *(Hyacinthaceae)*
Native to: Turkey, Syria
Bloom: Small, funnel-shaped flowers in abundant clusters; in red, pink, blue, violet, white, yellow, or apricot
Appearance: Winter-hardy bulb plant; erect growth, single-stemmed; with broad, linear leaves
Location: Sunny and warm; porous, moderately dry to moist soils rich in nutrients
Planting: Plant 4–6 in./10–16 cm deep in the fall
Care: Cover during the winter in cold areas; remove wilted parts; transplant every couple of years to keep the plants vital.
Arrangement: Plant in small groups in beds or in sunny edges of wooded areas, for example with *Iberis, Primula, Stachys byzantina, Viola,* and wild tulips
Notes: Blooms have a strong, sweet fragrance; good cut flowers
Species/Varieties: Gipsy Queen (apricot, → illus.); Carnegie (white), City of Haarlem (light yellow), Delft Blue (blue-purple), Ostara (blue), Lady Derby (pink), Pink Pearl (dark pink)

Height:
*4–8 inches/
10–20 cm*
**Blooming
Time:**
Feb.–March

Iris reticulata

Reticulata Iris

Family: Iris plants *(Iridiceae)*
Native to: Turkey, Iraq, Iran, Caucasus
Bloom: Relatively large blooms in blue-violet or light blue
with yellow and white markings
Appearance: Winter-hardy bulb plant with erect stems and
narrow, square, basal leaves; spreads slowly by means of bulbils
Location: Sunny and sheltered; very porous, even sandy soils
rich in nutrients; drier in the summer
Planting: Plant about 2 in./5 cm deep in the fall
Care: Best to let it simply grow in peace
Arrangement: Appropriate to sunny beds with neighbors that
don't grow too lush, for example *Allium, Dianthus, Iberis,
Santolina,* and *Stachys*
Notes: The blooms have a light fragrance.
Species/Varieties: Cantab (light blue, orange spots), Pauline
(violet with white), Springtime (dark blue with white); *L.
dangordiae* (yellow flowers with green dots, fragrant, for
warm, sunny, porous soils containing lime)

Height:
6–8 inches/
15–20 cm
Blooming Time:
Feb.–April

Leucojum vernum

Spring Snowflakes ✿

Family: Amaryllis plants *(Amaryllidaceae)*
Native to: Central and Eastern Europe
Bloom: White, nodding bellflowers with yellow-green tips
Appearance: Winter-hardy bulb plant; single-stemmed, erect growth; narrow, linear leaves that recede after blooming
Location: Partial to full shade and cool; moist to damp soils rich in nutrients that never dry out completely and ideally contain loam or clay; in appropriate locations, propagates by means of bulbils
Planting: Plant 3–4 in./8–10 cm deep in the fall
Care: No care required
Arrangement: Plant in several small groups, for example with *Epimedium, Fritillaria meleagris, Hyacinthoides,* and *Scilla*
Notes: Blooms smell like honey; bulb and foliage are poisonous.
Species/Varieties: *L. vernum* ssp. *carpaticum* (white with yellow tips); Summer Snowflake, *L. aestivum* (12–20 in./ 30–50 cm, May–June, branched), Gravetye Giant variety (large-flowered)

Height:
*31–59 inches/
80–150 cm*
**Blooming
Time:**
June–Sept.

L

Lilium Hybrids

Lily

Family: Lily plants *(Liliaceae)*
Bloom: Red, pink, yellow, or white bowls or trumpets in panicles; often spotted, and with flower petals that bend back
Appearance: Winter-hardy bulb plant; sturdy, erect growth; shiny, narrow to broad, lanceolate foliage
Location: Sun to partial shade; damp soils rich in nutrients that are still porous and free of standing water
Planting: Best planted 4–8 in./10–20 cm deep in a sandhill in the early fall; spread out the roots
Care: In the year of planting and in cold areas, always provide winter cover; stake if necessary
Arrangement: Place in small groups with *Delphinium, Echinacea, Leucanthemum, Phlox,* and *Rudbeckia*
Notes: Cut the blooms when the buds show color
Species/Varieties: Numerous varieties and types: Madonna Lily, *L. candidum* (39 in./100 cm, white, strong fragrance, June, likes lime, plant the bulbs just a little deeper than 1 in./3 cm); Martagon Lily, *L. martagon* (32 in./80 cm, pink, white, red, lavender, or yellow, May–June)

Height:
*6–10 inches/
15–25 cm*
**Blooming
Time:**
April–May

Muscari armeniacum

Grape Hyacinth ✿

Family: Hyacinth plants *(Hyacinthaceae)*
Native to: Balkans, Turkey
Bloom: Small, blue, white-rimmed or pure white bellflowers in thick clusters
Appearance: Winter-hardy bulb plant with grass-like foliage that recedes in the summer and grows in the fall
Location: Sunny and warm; moderately dry to moist, porous soils rich in nutrients
Planting: Plant 2–4 in./5–10 cm deep in the fall
Care: Remove leaves when they turn yellow
Arrangement: Goes wild with the help of bulbils; attractive with *Primula*, wild tulips, *Origanum* Thumbles Variety
Notes: Slightly poisonous; blooms are good for cutting
Species/Varieties: Alba (white), Blue Spike (blue, double), Cantab (sky blue), Early Giant (early bloomer); *M. botryoides* var. *botryoides* (8 in./20 cm, sky blue, April–May, broader leaves); *M. comosum* (8–12 in./20–30 cm, feather-like, blue-violet flowers, May–June, also in white)

Height:
*12–24 inches/
30–60 cm*
**Blooming
Time:**
March–May

N

Narcissus pseudonarcissus

Daffodil ✿
Also Known as: Narcissus

Family: Narcissus plants *(Amaryllidaceae)*
Native to: British Isles, France, Iberian Peninsula, Switzerland, Germany
Bloom: Yellow, white, orange trumpets; single or double
Appearance: Winter-hardy bulb plant; clustered growth; linear leaves that recede in June and July
Location: Sun to partial shade; on loose, humusy, moderately dry to moist soils rich in nutrients
Planting: Plant 4–6 in./10–15 cm deep in the fall
Care: Remove leaves when they turn yellow
Arrangement: Plant in small groups with yellow and blue flowers, for example with *Brunnera, Doronicum,* and *Polemonium*
Notes: The sap from the plant is a skin irritant. The blooms are cut for the vase in bud form.
Species/Varieties: Many varieties and types, for example *N. cyclamineus* (small trumpets); *N. jonquilla* (multiple blooms, very fragrant); *N. tazetta* (small bunches of blooms)

Height:
4–12 inches/
10–30 cm
**Blooming
Time:**
April–May

Ornithogalum umbellatum

Star of Bethlehem
**Also Known as: Sleepydick, Summer Snowflake, Starflower,
Pyrenees Star of Bethlehem**

Family: Hyacinth plants *(Hyacinthaceae)*
Native to: Europe, Turkey
Bloom: White starflowers with green outer stripe; multiple
blooms in loose umbels that open only at midday
Appearance: Winter-hardy bulb plant; grass-like bunches of
leaves that quickly recede after blooming; goes wild through
seeding and bulbils
Location: Sun to partial shade and warm; fairly dry soil, but
also thrives on any normal garden soil that's not too damp
Planting: Plant 3–4 in./8–10 cm deep in the fall
Care: No care required
Arrangement: Plant in several small groups, for example with
Nepeta, Origanum, Salvia, Stachys byzantina, and *Teucrium*
Notes: The entire plant is poisonous.
Species/Varieties: Nodding Star, *O. nutans* (16 in./40 cm,
nodding blooms, April–May, also grows in the shade)

Height:
*4–6 inches/
10–15 cm*
**Blooming
Time:**
April–May

P

    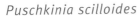

Puschkinia scilloides

Squill ✿

Family: Hyacinth plants *(Hyacinthaceae)*
Native to: Caucasus, Turkey
Bloom: Small, pale blue to white bells with dark blue outer stripe; multiple blooms in clusters that resemble small hyacinths
Appearance: Winter-hardy bulb plant; shiny, grass-like leaves that recede after blooming; propagates through self-seeding and bulbils
Location: Sun to partial shade and warm; also tolerates hot locations; any normal soil that's not too wet or dry
Planting: Plant 3–4 in./8–10 cm deep in the fall
Care: Remove leaves when they turn yellow
Arrangement: Very prone to going wild; plant with such flowers as *Chionodoxa, Iris, Leucojum, Scilla,* and *Viola*
Notes: The blooms are slightly fragrant.
Species/Varieties: Alba (white); Striped Squill, *P. Scilloides* var. *libanotica* (smaller flowers in white)

Height:
*4–6 inches/
10–15 cm*
**Blooming
Time:**
March–May

Scilla siberica

Siberian Squill ✿

Family: Hyacinth plants *(Hyacinthaceae)*
Native to: Russia, Turkey, Southwest Asia, Southern Europe
Bloom: Small, blue or white, nodding, star-shaped flowers in
clusters; dark stripes on the outside of the petals
Appearance: Winter-hardy bulb plant with broad, linear
leaves in bunches, from which grow two or three flower
shoots; propagates mainly through self-seeding
Location: Sun to partial shade and warm; on normal, humusy
garden soils; likes sunshine in the spring
Planting: Plant 2–4 in./5–10 cm deep in the fall; place close
together
Care: Best to let it grow undisturbed
Arrangement: Likes to go wild along the edge of deciduous
trees; attractive with *Bergenia, Brunnera, Crocus, Epimedium,
Eranthis, Galanthus, Lamium, Tiarella,* and wild tulips
Species/Varieties: Spring Beauty (larger, dark blue blooms,
sterile, propagates only through bulbils, → illus.), Atrocaerulea
(blue-violet); *S. bifolia* (4–6 in./10–15 cm, Feb.–March,
smaller and showier)

Height:
*12–28 inches/
30–70 cm*
**Blooming
Time:**
March–May

Tulipa Hybrids
Tulip

Family: Lily plants *(Liliaceae)*
Bloom: Single to fully double flower calyx in all colors except blue; also multicolored and patterned; with smooth, pointed, fringed, or wavy flower petals
Appearance: Winter-hardy bulb plant; broad, elliptical, pointed leaves that recede after blooming; usually single-stemmed
Location: Sun to partial shade and warm; porous soils rich in nutrients
Planting: Plant about 4 in./10 cm deep in the fall
Care: Cut off leaves when they turn yellow
Arrangement: Goes well in mixed beds, for example with *Bellis, Brunnera, Doronicum, Myosotis, Polemonium,* and Narcissus
Notes: Cut buds for the vase; poisonous
Species/Varieties: Lily-flowered Tulip (→ illus.; 16–28 in./ 40–70 cm, narrow blooms); Parrot Tulip (often bicolor, incised margins); Viridiflora Tulip (bicolor, with green stripes); Triumph Tulip (one- and two-colored); *T. tarda* (4–6 in./10–15 cm, yellow, April)

Plant Arrangements

Now on to some creative arrangements for the flowerbed. A couple of simple tricks can turn your garden into a treat for the eyes that will bloom as long and profusely as possible.

Arranging by Mood

Of course, you can simply take your favorite plants and place them anywhere in the bed. The result may turn out to be entirely appropriate. However, a planting is even more attractive with at least a little planning. The advantages are clear: a skillful combination allows the varieties to complement and highlight one another in blooming times, shapes, and colors.

Stylistic Unity: House and Garden

One point that deserves attention is the harmonious connection between house and garden. A fairly simple, modern façade is best complemented by a formal garden style (→ Technical

EXTRA TIP

A Plan Is Helpful
Draw a plan of your beds; let each plant be represented by a circle. Copy this pattern for each month, and then color in the flowering varieties or ornamental foliage that will be showing color. This will easily show if there are times when the bed will be lacking in color or flowers.

Terms). The picture is then determined by clear lines, geometric shapes, and selected plants with conspicuous shapes.

On the other hand, a house that radiates country rusticity fits with a farm garden or an English country garden (→ Technical Terms). Here, too, the beds are laid out in a geometric pattern; but they are filled with lush, multicolored perennials and summer plants. Usually these beds are backed up against a trimmed hedge and are

Skillful combinations result in long-lasting blooming.

> **Adapt the planting of the beds to the style of the garden.**

laid out in specific colors and shapes.

A natural-looking garden with soft, flowing lines goes well with a wood house. The choice of plants in this case depends on the location, rather than vice-versa, and the plants are allowed to go their own way.

It is attractive when the materials of the building are repeated in the garden in the form of walkways, seats, arbors, or garden houses.

Planting Patterns

Once you have identified the proper location with favorable light and soil conditions, the appropriate style, and the shape of the bed, you must now decide on a planting pattern.

You can plant the individual types in drifts or narrow bands. This is a favored method, especially with perennial beds. In any case, the bed must be sufficiently deep (at least 5 feet/1.5 m). To provide some variety with this pattern, you can occasionally place individual plants or rounded tufts in between. If you want a more sedate pattern, choose a unified, broad planting with ground covers from which small groups of taller perennials stand up.

What and Where to Plant

Most beds have a front and a back where they abut a wall or a hedge. It seems only logical that the tallest plants be placed toward the rear, with increasingly shorter ones toward the edge of the bed. But it is also possible to place taller plants in the center to create some unexpected views.

Some plants bloom early in the year and recede shortly thereafter; in other words, their stems and leaves turn yellow. Then they generally are cut back, resulting in empty spots.

Obviously, these species, such as Leopardbane or Oriental Poppy, are not appropriate for the front of the bed. They are best placed in the center or farther toward the back.

Perennials that bloom in the late summer or fall are placed toward the front, for they look nice even before they bloom. But this calls for types that don't grow especially tall, such as Stonecrop and Bushy Aster.

In addition, there are plants that are best for edging or framing the bed because of their wintergreen or evergreen foliage. Some

Tall plants usually are placed in the rear of the bed.

of them, such as Lavender Cotton and Germander, will even tolerate trimming to shape—in other words, they can be trimmed to form small hedges or geometric shapes.

Providing Bed Structure

Perennials and bulb and tuber plants continually change in the course of a year. Summer flowers are set out in May and are cleaned up in the fall. So it's desirable if all this inconstancy also includes a couple of enduring eyecatchers. These may be grasses that are cut back in the spring when the new growth begins, such as Feather Reed Grass (*Calamagrostis × acutiflora* Karl Foerster), Switch Grass (*Panicum virgatum*), or Maiden Grass (*Miscanthus*).

Evergreen plants are also known quantities. Small shrubs such as Boxwood are suitable; it looks best when trimmed to shape (e.g., in a ball or a pyramid).

Perennials such as Bergenia and Coralbells, with their beautiful foliage, belong among the consistent features. Oftentimes they step into the limelight in the winter, when the conspicuous blooming plants

Plant Arrangements

1 Decorative: Daylilies

2 Exciting color accents

3 Provide contrasting shapes among the flowers.

4 Contrasting foliage

Veil effect: Purpletop Verbena **5**

are on their way out. The impressive, long-lasting inflorescences of Delphinium and Globe Thistle can also serve as a focal point for a while.

In Eyecatching Company

Another element that provides structure is the balanced use of specimen, companion, and filler plants.

A specimen plant is distinguished by a particularly noteworthy bloom, ornamental foliage, or attractive growth. They are placed in the bed singly in a more or less regular pattern, or in groups. The size of the groups can vary to keep the planting dynamic. It is also possible to use varieties that remain attractive as long as possible, such as Sage, Stonecrop, and Chinese Peony. After blooming, one specimen plant can also cede "leadership" to another. So, for example, Oriental Poppy can be combined with Fernleaf Yarrow. When the Poppy goes by in June, the Yarrow takes over the duty seamlessly—but in a different flower color!

The specimen plants are accompanied by companion plants and filler plants. The specimen plants keep the concept together, even if the individual companion and filler plants vary. For example, if you choose Delphinium as a specimen plant, you can place a couple of Daylilies with one Delphinium group, and place some Bellflowers with the next one. The important thing is that the neighbors grow shorter or as ground cover. The symbols in the plant portraits will quickly indi-

EXTRA TIP

Setting up Contrasts
When you combine plants, make sure that plants that are as visually dissimilar as possible grow next to one another:
➤ **Contrasting growth:** Place long, erect plants next to stocky, bushy, or bulky ones with a clear outline.
➤ **Contrasting shapes:** For example, set grass-like foliage next to round or heart-shaped leaves.

cate which plants are appropriate for which application. The following guidelines are useful for intensive plantings:

➤ **Specimen Perennials:** one to three plants for every square yard/meter

➤ **Companion Perennials:** three to seven plants per square yard/meter

➤ **Filler Perennials:** seven to ten plants per square yard/meter

➤ **Annuals and Biennials** need less root space; they can be placed almost twice as closely together.

➤ **Bulbs** generally are set about an inch/a coule of centimeters apart from one

> **Here's what the recommended planting looks like in early summer.**

another. Large varieties such as Dahlias, which need more space, are an exception.

To avoid losing perspective in planning your flowerbed, it's best to procede in this way:

➤ Shrubs come first in the bed. They usually are larger and more dominant than the other plants.

➤ Next come the specimen plants, or else the largest perennials.

➤ The companion and filler plants are matched up with the specimen plants.

➤ Finally, the bulb plants are sprinkled in.

➤ Summer flowers can be planned in advance, according to their qualities as specimen, companion, or filler plants. Or else they can be simply plugged into any resulting empty spots. That's also how to fill in a bed whenever an unforeseen empty spot crops us, for example if one plant doesn't make it.

Whether delicate or robust, grasses enrich every flowerbed.

PLANTING RECOMMENDATION

Bed size: 6 × 15 feet/5 × 2 m
Location: sun, normal soil

➤ **Jerusalem Sage** (*Phlomis russeliana*), yellow: three individual plants

➤ **Milky Bellflower** (*Campanula lactiflora* Loddon Anne), soft pink: three groups of two plants

➤ **May Night Sage** (*Salvia nemorosa* May Night), purple: three groups of three plants

➤ **Magnificent Geranium** (*Geranium magnificium*), dark violet: two groups of three plants

➤ **Armenian Cranesbill** (*G. psilostemon*), pink: two groups of two plants

➤ **Tufted Pansy** (*Viola cornuta* Boughton Blue), blue: two groups of five plants

➤ **Coralbells** (*Heuchera micrantha* Palace Purple), red-brown foliage: two groups of three plants

➤ **Switch Grass** (*Panicum virgatum* Squaw), pink flower heads, red coloration in the fall: three groups of one plant each

Colors and Shapes Throughout the Year

The ideal flowerbed presents an attractive appearance year-round. This doesn't mean that the entire bed needs to bloom without interruption. Many times a few leaves with attractive markings and shapes, or a charming arrangement, are all that's needed.

Attractive Year-round

Setting up a bed to last throughout the year is simplest when just one plant group is used, rather than combining perennials, annuals, biennials, and bulb plants in the bed.

> **A flowerbed containing only summer blooms is attractive for just a limited time.**

A bed with only summer flowers would appear in blazing color from June to September, but in the rest of the months it would be bare and unsightly. The problem with bulb flowers is that individual species bloom in every season, but they only show themselves in the best form through a usually brief high point. For when the blooms go by, the leaves also recede. Without perennials, then, in many respects, there is nothing that goes into a bed that shines without leaving any empty spots among the flowers. The perennials complement the annuals and biennials while they are in bloom and fill in during the time when there are no summer flowers. Along with the spring bulbs, perennials show the first patches of color, and later in the year they cover up the unattractive leaves of the spring bulbs. In such mixed beds, small shrubs—especially ones that can be trimmed to shape—can also be included.

Once you have decided on your plants, use a monthly plan to check as accurately as possible whether your bed will show its best side all year long, or if there will be times when there is a lack of blooming plants (→ Extra Tip, p. 232).

Plant by Color!

Another possibility is to go by a specific color scheme. The flower colors are surely the most conspicuous part of any plant.

Colors affect our feelings and also influence the spatial effect of a flowerbed.

The color circle works wonderfully for locating appropriate color groups for flowerbeds. It is the product of arranging the colors of

PLANTING RECOMMENDATIONS

Bed size: 9 × 9 feet/ 3 × 3 m
Location: sun, average soil

VARIANT 1
➤ **Dahlia** (*Dahlia* hybrid), dark pink, no forms that look like Zinnias: three individual plants
➤ **Zinnia** (*Zinnia elegans* Envy Double), yellow-green: four groups of three plants
➤ **Beard Tongue** (*Penstemon* hybrid Lilac Purple), red-violet: three groups of three plants
➤ **Verbena** (*Verbena hastata*): sow randomly

VARIANT 2
➤ **Marigold**, orange, double: three groups of three plants
➤ **Painted Nettle** (*Solenostemon scutellarioides* Sedona): four individual plants
➤ **Sulfur Cosmos**: three groups of three plants
➤ **Feverfew Golden Moss**: three groups of three plants
➤ **Coralbells** (*Heuchera* Amber Waves), orange yellow leaves: four groups of two plants

light as they appear in a rainbow. The colors that lie directly opposite one another (e.g., yellow and violet), exhibit the strongest contrasts, and thus go together very well. Hues lying next to one another, such as orange and red, work together harmoniously, and thus are a good match for one another. Harmonies always produce a relaxing effect on the eye, whereas contrasts are lively and stimulating.

In addition, colors have different 'temperatures": red and yellow are connected to warmth, whereas blue emanates coolness. All mixtures in which red or yellow predominate thus seem warmer than ones with a lot of blue.

This "temperature" plays a major role in the spatial effect of a flowerbed: optically, all warm colors crowd toward the foreground, while cool hues appear to pull back. So narrow beds can be made to appear deeper and larger with a few blue flowers. Too much yellow or red, on the other hand, makes them appear even smaller than they are.

When you settle on a particular color scheme, you don't have to stick to it for

Hosta and ferns are the perfect complement to one another in shady locations.

the whole year. In mixed beds, the colors can be changed several times so that, for example, red and yellow predominate in the spring and give way to yellow and blue in the summer, and blue and red in the fall.

Leaves Instead of Flowers

In addition to flowers, the leaves of many strains exhibit multiple luminous colors. They provide new and interesting possibilities for arranging a flowerbed. In comparison to blooming time, they decorate a plant—at least in the case of perennials—for much longer. Plants such as Coralbells, which are still around even in the winter months, are particularly worthwhile. In this season, which in comparison to the others is devoid of flowers, they provide welcome areas of color.

PLANTING RECOMMENDATION

Bed size: 5 × 20 feet/ 4 × 1.5 m
Location: partial shade, average soil

➤ **Lenten Rose,** white: three individual plants
➤ **Astilbe** (*Astilbe japonica* Deutschland), white: two groups of three plants
➤ **Forget-Me-Not,** blue: two groups of two plants
➤ **Hosta** (*Hosta* Francee), white-spotted leaves: two plants
➤ **Bergenia** (*Bergenia* Silver Light), white: two groups of three plants
➤ **Solomon's Seal,** white: three groups of three plants
➤ **Foamflower,** white: two groups of three plants
➤ **Blue Lungwort** (*Pulmonaria angustifolia* Mawson), blue: two groups of three plants
➤ **Common Periwinkle** (*Vinca minor* Gertrude Jekyll), white: two groups of two plants
➤ Scatter in small tufts of five to nine plants of the following: Snowdrop, Siberian Squill, and Hardy Cyclamen

Plant Arrangements

Crocus	p. 211	Heliotrope	p. 189
Ageratum	p. 175	Pansy	p. 202
Toadflax	p. 118	Cranesbill	pp. 88, 90–92
Lily	p. 223	Daylily	p. 100
Daisy	p. 179	Tulip	p. 229
Daffodil	p. 225	Tufted Pansy	p. 171
Primrose	p. 145	Clematis	p. 67
Coralbells	p. 101	Meadow Rue	p. 162
Squill	p. 227	Hyssop	p. 30
Glory of the Snow	p. 207	Betony	p. 159
Var. Japanese Aster	p. 107		

SUNNY BED/DRY SOIL

Aster	pp. 40–45, 181	Mullein	p. 167
White Sage	p. 37	Globe Thistle	p. 77
Calamint	p. 55	Lavender	p. 112
Jerusalem Sage	p. 136	Toadflax	p. 118
Purple Oregano	p. 132	Colewort	p. 70
Stonecrop	p. 156	Sleepydick	p. 226
Cornflower	pp. 60, 61	Feathered Pink	pp. 72, 185
Lady's Mantle	p. 31	Adam's Needle	p. 173
Germander	p. 161	Pearly Everlasting	p. 32
Lavender Cotton	p. 153	Blazing Star	p. 115
Plumbago	p. 63	Baby's Breath	p. 95
Chamomile	p. 35	Cheddar Wood	p. 120
Iris	pp. 105, 106, 221	Sea Lavender	p. 117
Jacob's Rod	p. 39	Cranesbill	pp. 87–93
Catmint	pp. 128, 129	Spurge	pp. 82–84
Knautia	p. 109	Hyssop	p. 30
		Betony	p. 159

SUNNY BED/MOIST TO DAMP SOIL

Elecampane	p. 104	Torch Lily	p. 110
Culver's Root	p. 169	Fleabane	p. 79
Aster	pp. 41–45	Loosestrife	pp. 123, 124
Bergenia	p. 50	Foxglove	p. 74
Speedwell	p. 146	Lady's Mantle	p. 31
Spiderwort	p. 164	Goat's Beard	p. 38
Monkshood	p. 29	Rosy Spire	p. 140

Plant Arrangements

HALF-SHADY BED/MOIST TO DAMP SOIL

Foamflower	p. 163	Spotted Dead Nettle	p. 111
Coneflower	p. 76	Bleeding Heart	p. 73
Snowdrop	p. 217	Globe Flower	p. 166
Black Beauty	p. 66	Yellow Wax Bells	p. 108
Astrantia	p. 49	Barren Strawberry	p. 172
Pansy	p. 202	Joe-pye Weed	p. 81
Cranesbill	pp. 88, 90, 91, 93	Loosestrife	p. 125
		Bistorta amplexicaulis	p. 51
Day Lily	p. 100	Betony	p. 159

HALF-SHADY BED/DRY SOIL

Bergenia	p. 50	Sleepydick	p. 226
Calamint	p. 55	Cheddar Wood	p. 120
Lady's Mantle	p. 31	Cranesbill	pp. 87, 88, 90
Plumbago	p. 63		

SHADY BED/NORMAL SOIL

Fringe Cups	p. 160	Lily of the Valley	p. 208
Astilbe	pp. 46–48	Lenten Rose	p. 99
Bergenia	p. 50	Phlox	p. 137
Epimedium	p. 78	Solomon's Seal	p. 143
Lady's Mantle	p. 31	Rodgersia	p. 149
Hosta	p. 102	Snake's Head	p. 163
Creeping Forget-Me-Not	p. 131	Black Beauty	p. 66
		Barren Strawberry	p. 172
Bellflower	p. 57	Windflower	p. 206
Periwinkle	p. 170	Winter Aconite	p. 214
Lungwort	p. 147	Spurge	p. 82

SHADY BED/MOIST TO DAMP SOIL

Astilbe	pp. 46–48	Solomon's Seal	p. 143
Bergenia	p. 50	Rodgersia	p. 149
Epimedium	p. 78	Foamflower	p. 163
Lady's Mantle	p. 31	Black Beauty	p. 66
Bellflower	p. 57	Astrantia	p. 49
Hairy Toad Lily	p. 165	Spotted Dead Nettle	p. 111
Lily of the Valley	p. 208	Yellow Wax Bells	p. 108
Spring Snowflakes	p. 222	Barren Strawberry	p. 172

Plant Index

Page numbers in **bold type** refer to photos.

Appendix